ECONOMICALLY
SAVVY

YOUR PERSONAL GUIDE TO WEALTH AND FINANCIAL WELLNESS

2ND EDITION

TYWANQUILA WALKER

ISBN: 978-1-962242-03-5 (ebook)
ISBN: 978-1-962242-04-2 (paperback)
ISBN: 978-1-962242-05-9 (hardcover)

Library of Congress Control Number: 2023914850

Second Edition: October 2023

Publisher's Cataloging-in-Publication data

Names: Walker, Tywanquila, author.

Title: Economically savvy : your personal guide to wealth and financial wellness / Tywanquila Walker.

Description: 2nd edition. | Millington, TN: Tywanquila Walker, 2023.

Identifiers: LCCN: 2023914850 | ISBN: 978-1-962242-05-9 (hardcover) | 978-1-962242-04-2 (paperback) | 978-1-962242-03-5 (ebook)

Subjects: LCSH Financial planning. | Finance, Personal. | Investments. | BISAC BUSINESS & ECONOMICS / Personal Finance / Money Management | BUSINESS & ECONOMICS / Personal Finance / Budgeting

BUSINESS & ECONOMICS / Personal Finance / Retirement Planning | BUSINESS & ECONOMICS / Personal Finance / General | BUSINESS & ECONOMICS / Finance / Wealth Management

Classification: LCC HG179 .W35 2023 | DDC 332.02--dc23

orderyourlife.com

CONTENTS

INTRODUCTION

ECONOMICALLY SAVVY: YOUR MONEY
& YOUR MINDSET

If you know me well, you know I'm good at finding ways to save money. Do not call me dirty words like cheap, frugal, or tightfisted. I *will* take offense. Instead, I prefer a more sophisticated term – **economically savvy**.

Economic savviness is the art and science of finance combined with the wisdom of long-term planning. Economic savviness is fiscal. It is visionary. It is behavioral. It is personal.

To be economically savvy, you must rethink your relationship with money, determine your wants versus your needs, and embrace the tools and opportunities that make financial freedom possible. Becoming economically savvy is an evolution, one that begins with conscious effort and eventually becomes second nature.

This guide to economic savviness is written to provide maximum flexibility. Each chapter has a specific theme, which means you can read the chapters in order or select the chapters that are most relevant to your goals at this particular moment in your life.

In this book, you will learn about your money and the general principles of money management. I will introduce you to side hustles, money saving apps, and compound interest. I will also tackle tough financial topics such as debt and preparing for major life events – namely, college and retirement.

You will notice I mention apps, websites, and research multiple times throughout this book. I will constantly remind you of the technology that is literally at your fingertips. Free apps and websites exist to save you money. Information and technology that support your financial goals are readily available. Thus, Part I of *Economically Savvy* is all about money, and Part II is about teaching your children to become economically savvy.

Because achieving financial wellness requires behavioral changes and a focused mind, Part III is all about mindset. I am always in an economically savvy mindset. I want you to have an economically savvy mindset, too.

When our minds, homes, and hearts are cluttered, and our stress levels are elevated, it can be difficult to think clearly about our financial wellbeing. Hence, the latter chapters focus on shopping tips, simplifying your life, and handling tough situations. Making financial decisions can be difficult. Having a clear mind and a plan of action may alleviate some of the stress. You can do this.

Get ready to become economically savvy. Take a few moments to think about your goals to build wealth and live a life of financial wellness. To achieve your goals, you must have the right mindset. Work towards what you want and never give up.

Go forth and be economically savvy!

Dr. Tywanquila Walker

PART I:
THE MONEY

CHAPTER ONE

THREE BASIC PRINCIPLES OF MONEY MANAGEMENT

Are you at peace with your financial life? Given that money and work are major stressors for most adults, your answer may not come as a surprise.

Today, begin incorporating the three basic principles of money management into your life. The principles I discuss below are easy to follow. My instructions are simple.

Getting into financial hardship is easy. Getting out is easier than you think. Follow these principles and get your financial life in order.

1. Needs vs Wants

Know your priorities. Clearly distinguish between your needs and your wants.

Needs are life's essentials that you cannot live without – think food, water, and shelter.

Wants are things you wish for, or desire to have, but they are not essential for survival – think the latest phone, a luxury vehicle, or 200 pairs of shoes.

Yes, you need clothes. But do you need designer clothes? Yes, you need food. But do you need the most expensive steak on the menu?

There is nothing wrong with getting the things you want, as long as you have already thoroughly taken care of the things you need. Once you know the difference between your needs vs your wants, you can move on to basic money management principle number two.

2. Budgeting

Always have a budget. People who follow a budget are less likely to overspend.

If you often wonder where your money went, you find you don't have enough money to pay your bills, or your credit card balance is through the roof, you need a budget.

A budget is the key to your financial plan. It helps you keep track of your finances and your financial goals.

Begin your budget by writing down your total monthly income. What is your monthly salary? Do you have other income such as child support, alimony, a side hustle, or a part-time job?

Next, write out your total expenses. For example, how much do you pay for rent, mortgage, groceries, health insurance, or child care?

Finally, take your total income and subtract your total expenses (i.e., total income – total expenses) to find out how well you are doing with budgeting your income.

+ : If you get a positive number, good job! Your income is more than your expenses. You have money left to save (or spend on one of your wants).

- : If you get a negative number, get to work. Your expenses are more than your income. Look at your budget and find ways to cut your expenses or increase your income. Regularly evaluate your budget to ensure you are living within your means.

3. Savings and Emergency Funds

Always have an emergency fund. Life is full of unexpected events. You never know when you might need a major car repair, lose your job, have a medical emergency, or experience a death in the family. During these stressful times, your savings may be your savior.

If you do not have a savings account or an emergency fund, start one.

Build your fund by paying yourself first. In your budget, incorporate saving as a recurring expense. Similarly to paying your bills on a schedule, contribute to your savings on a schedule. Know that as soon as you receive income, a portion of it goes to your savings or emergency fund.

I mention savings and emergency funds together because you can choose to have one fund (e.g., an emergency fund) or you can have two funds (i.e., one for savings and one for emergencies).

If you are just starting out, begin with one fund. Put whatever you can in your emergency fund and do not touch the money unless you have a major emergency.

If you are more advanced, and your needs are thoroughly taken care of, consider having two funds. Build your emergency fund and use it for emergencies only. Build your savings fund and use it to save up for your wants (e.g., a vacation). If you decide to have two funds, make sure you contribute to them both; only use each fund for its designated purpose. For instance, if you do not have enough money in your savings fund, do not use your emergency fund to make up the difference so you can go on vacation. That is not what your emergency fund is for.

If you lack the discipline to have two funds, have one designated emergency fund. Only use the fund when you have an emergency.

You Can Do This

Achieving financial peace is easier than you think. When you know your needs, you are in a better position to develop a budget and save for your future. Once you master the three basic principles of money management, you will be better able to cope with a financial crisis.

Take your time. Learn as you go. Share your knowledge. You can do this!

CHAPTER TWO

NEED EXTRA MONEY?
GET A SIDE HUSTLE

Today it is time to wake up, refresh, and embrace the opportunity to better your life and the lives of those around you.

Today is the day to address your money matters and reflect upon the financial wellness goals you want to improve upon.

Would you like to save for a summer vacation? Do you have dreams of travelling the world? Do you need more money?

My answer to you is, "Get a side hustle!"

I have a side hustle. In truth, at any given time, I have 4 or 5 side hustles. As you will see from the lists below, I have participated in a lot of extracurricular activities. I've made thousands of dollars from my side hustles, all while maintaining my full-time job.

If something works, I stick with it. If not, I move on. That's the beauty of side hustles – ultimate flexibility with minimum commitment and maximum earnings.

My Side Hustles Present

Couponing and Cash Back – Most people know I coupon and look for ways to earn cash back. I will talk more about my couponing journey in later chapters. Just know that once I started couponing, I never looked backed.

Adjunct Professor (Online) – I like to stay up-to-date on recent research and technological advancements. I also have a PhD and I like to put it to use. One of the best ways to keep learning is to teach, so I do. I teach online and serve as the dissertation chair for PhD candidates. Teaching online provides me the flexibility to work when I want and it gives me the opportunity to shape young minds. As an added bonus, my university offers a retirement plan. Given that I teach part-time, I don't earn much, but every penny towards retirement adds to my bottom line.

User Testing – Testing websites and apps for companies is one of my easiest side hustles. Where else can I get paid to talk and give my opinions? There are dozens of user testing companies out there. The one I use is called UserTesting (easy to remember, right). I usually spend a few minutes a day searching for tests. I won't get rich as a tester, but I like adding money to my savings account.

Start a Business – For me, Order Your Life (OrderYourLife. com) is part side hustle, part full-time obsession, part my future and my life. Although Order Your Life has not made me a millionaire (yet), I enjoy the challenge of being a business owner. What other vocation affords me the opportunity to make my own schedule while continuously learning new skills? (To be clear, I have a full-time job in addition to Order Your Life. Balance is one of those skills I'm continuously learning.)

Make T-shirts (aka Start a Second Business) – I have a confession – I have a second business. I sell t-shirts online. Although technically a side hustle, Shirts Because (https://tinyurl. com/shirtsbecause) is actually a hobby. Designing is calming and relaxing, so I dabble in my (limited) spare time. Shirts Because is my no-pressure pastime. I design when inspiration strikes, and I make a few extra dollars.

My Side Hustles Past

Freelance Editor – I have worked as a freelance editor for a company and as an independent freelancer. When working for the company, the pay was great and the work was steady. However, over time, I learned that the company was shady and the upper management was downright rude. I stopped providing freelance services to the company, which decreased my side hustle income but made me feel good about having morals. I still provide editing services when asked. Nevertheless, because I don't edit on a continuous basis, freelance editing is an occasional side hustle that most appropriately fits under my past.

Fiverr (http://www.fiverr.com/s2/d100ce524b) – I'm not quite sure if Fiverr belongs in my present, my past, or my future. Every few months, I reactivate my Fiverr gigs. When I have down time or I'm off work during a holiday, I open my Fiverr gigs for business. I've earned a few extra dollars on Fiverr, so it will likely remain on my list of occasional side hustles.

Online Surveys – I used to do online surveys. I would set a goal then complete enough tasks to cash out. I enjoyed doing surveys. However, I have found other, more lucrative side hustles.

My Sides Hustles Future

Consulting – When people find out I own a business, they are full of questions. They want to know about best practices, startup costs, taxes, marketing and advertising, and generally how to get started. People also ask financial questions. For example, how do I save money? How do I plan for retirement? How do I buy a house? How do I find scholarships for college?

The more questions I answer, the more I think about charging for my services.

According to Kim Garst, "If you don't value your time, neither will others. Stop giving away your time and talents. Value what you know and start charging for it." Here's my bill…

51 Side Hustles That May Work for You

Do any of the side hustles above strike your fancy?

There are dozens of possible side hustles out there. Find the ones that work for you.

Here is a list of 51 side hustles that might interest you. Most of these activities you can do on your own, with little to no startup costs. The main objective is to charge for your skills and services. What skills do you have that someone else needs? Make it a side hustle.

1. Edit or proofread documents
2. Write (e.g., become a freelance writer or a ghostwriter)
3. Create professional presentations
4. Sell handmade art, jewelry, or furniture
5. Become a virtual assistant
6. Cook or bake
7. Babysit
8. Plan parties and other social events
9. Test websites, apps, or video games (i.e., become a user tester)
10. Blog
11. Tutor
12. Teach

13. Sing, play music, or DJ at events

14. Present or lecture (on your favorite topics)

15. Clean (for friends, family, or businesses)

16. Organize physical (or digital) spaces

17. Install software

18. Create social media posts

19. Fix computers, phones, or other devices

20. Set up social media accounts

21. Make or design t-shirts

22. Check in on apps

23. Coupon

24. Clean carpets

25. Mow lawns or provide yard work services

26. Run errands for other people

27. Pet sit

28. Walk dogs

29. Write or edit resumes

30. Become a consultant

31. Create scrapbooks or photo albums (these can be physical or digital)

32. Become a photographer (of landscapes, family portraits, or ecommerce products)

33. Become a videographer

34. Become a personal assistant

35. Sell items online

36. Sell items at garage sales or flea markets

37. Drive for a rideshare company

38. Become a social media manger

39. Wash and detail cars

40. Give music lessons

41. House sit

42. Do online surveys

43. Wash, iron, or fold laundry

44. Become a fitness or dance instructor

45. Design websites

46. Make deliveries

47. Become a handyman or handywoman

48. Help people move

49. Become a tour guide

50. Become a freelance bookkeeper, accountant, or tax preparer

51. Do whatever you're good at on Fiverr, Upwork, TaskRabbit, Time etc, Etsy (https://etsy.me/3Xi6P2m), or another online platform or worksite.

CHAPTER THREE

SAVE MONEY ON THE THINGS
YOU ALREADY BUY

Now that you are familiar with money management and side hustles, let me share with you all the tips and tricks I have picked up over the years. First, let's begin with a brief history of my journey to economic savviness.

1. The Journey

As far back as I can remember, I was the child who liked to save everything. For example, I liked to eat my Halloween candy over the course of days (or weeks), instead of all in one day. I saved my pennies until I could buy something at the store I really wanted. I collected my baseball cards instead of trading each one for a cheap toy. I hung onto those little carnival tickets until I had enough for the prize I wanted. When people asked, "How'd you get that?" I just shrugged and smiled.

As an adult, my habits haven't changed much. I'm not a hoarder, and I don't keep things I don't need. However, I do have a knack for hanging on to things until I can upscale them for something bigger and better. After minimizing the costs of my everyday expenses, I use the savings to buy things I really want (e.g., a vacation, a new tv, or an upgrade to my 13-year-old car).

The psychological term is delayed gratification. When it comes to money, I call it economic savviness.

What does it take to become economically savvy?

2. Minimize the Costs of Your Everyday Expenses

One of the easiest ways to become economically savvy is to save money on the things you buy every day. Food, personal hygiene products, and cleaning supplies are some of the easiest things to save on. Do you need to buy toilet paper, deodorant, or snacks for a party? Whenever you can, buy these items when they are on sale. What do you do when there isn't a sale? There's a coupon, or an app, for that.

I started couponing and using apps years ago when I accepted a new job but, for practical reasons, I needed to leave the old job while I moved and waited for the new one to begin. I knew it would be a few months before my job started (to be exact, there were 5 months between the time I accepted the job offer and the day I actually started working).

I was financially secure, with a healthy savings account and no car notes or loans. I'd even managed to make a few extra bucks by selling some of my stuff. However, being the economically savvy person I am, I was not willing to spend one more penny than I needed to. Thus, I began couponing and using apps.

3. Use Those Coupons

Couponing is fun and challenging. When I started, I used two of my favorite websites, The Krazy Coupon Lady and Hip2Save, to get started. These ladies have got the details of couponing covered. They discuss everything, including how to save the most at your favorite stores.

Additionally, Collin of Hip2Save has a great video about creating a coupon binder. Although I mostly use apps now, my coupon binder is still an important part of my economic savviness. Sometimes, the best coupons are only available in print. I use every resource available to save money.

4. There Is an App for That

If you don't believe you have time to clip coupons, or you want to search for coupons while you're in the store, there are apps for that. Above, I only mentioned two of my favorite websites. However, there are hundreds of bloggers, small businesses, and large corporations that offer coupons and money-saving apps.

It's likely your favorite grocery store, your favorite brand of toilet paper, and your favorite restaurant offer coupons through an app.

Money-saving apps have come a long way since I began couponing. I have tried over a dozen couponing apps. Some of the app companies experienced long slow deaths and no longer exist. Some have merged with other companies. Still others have changed their names and become different types of apps. Through all the ups and downs, here is a list of my four top-rated money-saving apps (of the moment).

- Ibotta (https://ibotta.com/r/nghfxmq)
- Rakuten (https://www.rakuten.com/r/TAICHI95)
- Shopkick (https://get.shopkick.com/96Rn/mdfyp1xr)
- Fetch Rewards (https://tinyurl.com/3ce2vtr3)

5. Go Slowly

Take your time on your economic savviness journey. If you try to rush, or you believe you will get rich overnight, you will get frustrated and end a really fruitful voyage. If you feel overwhelmed by all the choices above, choose one app or one website and stick with it.

I started out searching only one website for coupons I needed immediately. Then, I began searching multiple websites and saving coupons for future purchases. Eventually, I made a coupon binder.

Next, I downloaded one app, then two, then three. Now, I consistently use eight money-saving apps. I have others, but I only use them when I need specific items. I've also signed up for email alerts from my favorite household brands.

To keep my inbox from getting cluttered, I've set up my email to mark those messages as read and automatically send them to a specific email folder. I open the folder when I need the coupons. Otherwise, I ignore the emails.

As you can see, it has taken me a long time to develop a couponing system that works for me. Take your time, and you will find out what works for you.

With a little effort, you can become economically savvy, too.

6. Share the Knowledge

When I started, I kept a log of how much I saved with each shopping trip and sent bragworthy snapshots of my receipts to friends and family. When I have a really good grocery haul or I get a lot of items for free, I still send out pictures of my receipts. I also send out alerts when I find coupons or sales that others would appreciate. I have even taken friends and family members to the store with me so they can see how to double and triple stack coupons.

There are a lot of people who want to save money. Share your knowledge with them.

CHAPTER FOUR

MONEY SAVING APPS AND WEBSITES

On my phone, I have a group of apps that are exclusively dedicated to saving me money. I have moved these apps to a folder (i.e., that amazing option that lets you organize your home screen and group similar apps together). My folder is appropriately named $. Yep, it's a dollar sign.

Happy Saving!

Here is a list of the apps and websites I use most often.

Disclaimer: For some of these apps, if you use my referral code, I get a little change in my pocket. A few of the apps (e.g., Ibotta and Uber), offer you a little change, too. Cha-Ching!

I save money by using the apps, and I make money by sharing my referral codes.

After you download the apps, share your referral codes, too. Sharing is caring – and economically savvy.

Ibotta

Use my referral code and you can earn a signup bonus. To receive your bonus, redeem a rebate within 7 days of registration. "Any Brand" and "Any Item" rebates are excluded and do not count toward the bonus; you must redeem a product rebate.

Invite link: https://ibotta.com/r/nghfxmq

Referral code: **NGHFXMQ**

Rakuten

Sign up with my invite link to receive a bonus. To receive your bonus, within 90 days of becoming a member, you must make qualifying purchases totaling at least $25.

Invite link: https://www.rakuten.com/r/TAICHI95

Fetch Rewards

Use my referral code during signup and you'll get bonus points when you scan your first receipt.

Invite link: https://tinyurl.com/3ce2vtr3

Referral code: **PG4VK**

Shopkick

To get your bonus, use my referral code when you sign up. Then, within 7 days, complete a walk-in, scan a receipt, or earn 25 kicks by scanning products while you're in a store. Shopkick offers many ways to earn kicks (without the obligation to buy anything).

Invite link: https://get.shopkick.com/96Rn/mdfyp1xr

Referral code: BEST220294

Uber

Use my referral code and get money towards a free ride.

Invite link: https://www.uber.com/invite/tw2570ue

Referral code: **TW2570UE**

Coupons.com and RetailMeNot

I do not have referral codes for Coupons.com and RetailMeNot. However, they are two great money saving apps to have in your economically savvy arsenal.

Grocery Store and Retailer Apps

Download the apps to your favorite stores and use their digital coupons. Maximize your savings by combining the deals offered at your favorite stores with the deals offered in money saving apps. You'll be surprised by how much you can save on the things you already buy.

CHAPTER FIVE

HOW MUCH MONEY CAN YOU MAKE USING APPS?

In the previous chapters, I described my journey to economic savviness and gave you numerous tips to help you on this voyage. One of those tips was about money saving apps. Now, I am going to tell you how much money I've made, or saved, using apps.

Full Disclosure

There are a lot of people who list the apps they use and their referral codes. However, very few people are willing to disclose how much they've made using apps. When I first started couponing, I wanted to know if the apps people were suggesting were worth my while.

Would I make any money? How long had they been using the apps? Did they actually use the apps that were presented on their websites? Most of the time, my questions were not answered. All I found were referral links.

I believe in transparency, so I'll answer the last question first. Yes, I use all the money saving apps I mention in this book. As for how much money I've made and how long I've been using each app, see the numbers below.

The numbers include my top performing apps. Keep in mind that I also save money with store apps and coupons. These savings can be harder to track, unless I spend a lot of time recording every single transaction. And who has time for that?

The best apps show me how much I've saved over time. As you can see, for me, some apps have more earning potential than others.

The Numbers

I have made $800.91 with Ibotta (since 2015), $698.53 with Rakuten (since 2017), $277.56 with Target Circle (since 2014), $200 with mPlus Rewards (since 2015), $42.10 with SavingStar (since 2017), and $60 with Fetch Rewards (since 2017). That's over $2000 from these six apps alone. It may not sound like much, but that's money I can put in my emergency fund or use for something else.

Sadly, mPlusRewards and SavingStar no longer exist. However, SavingStar merged with Coupons.com and continues to live on, albeit under a different name.

And the Winner Is…

Ibotta is clearly the winner for me. Even when I don't buy an item on their list of many options, there is usually an "any item" cash back offer available. Over time, those 25¢ rebates add up.

As an economically savvy connoisseur, I believe every penny counts. It takes pennies to makes dollars.

CHAPTER SIX

SAVING, THE DIRTY WORD
NOBODY WANTS TO HEAR

Why do people cringe when I tell them they need to save? How many of us are guaranteed to win the lottery, inherit a multimillion-dollar estate, or meet a billionaire who is willing to adopt us and support us for the rest of our lives?

If you are one of those people, I think I'm your long-lost cousin. If you are not one of those people, keep reading and save along with me.

1. Have a Savings Goal

To be a successful saver, you must have a savings goal. First, decide what you are saving for. Do you need a new car or want to buy your dream home? Are you building a college fund for your child? Do you want to finally be able to take a vacation? Is your family starting an emergency fund?

Whatever your reason for saving, think about it, commit to it, and write it down. Have you written it down? Good. Now it's time to write down how much you plan to save.

Do you need to save $50? A few hundred dollars? A few thousand dollars? Write it down.

How often, and how much, will you save? Depending on my savings goal, I like to save money in different places at different times. For example, money goes into my retirement account every two weeks. In contrast, I usually put money into my savings account every month. Although the amount deposited into my savings account changes as my life and goals change (e.g., going on vacation vs buying a car), contributions to my retirement account are steady and unchanging.

A vacation or a car is a short-term goal, while retirement is a long-term goal. It is okay to have multiple savings goals. The key is to write down your timelines and keep the funds separate. For example, I don't plan to touch my retirement money until I'm at least 100. Okay, that is a bit of an exaggeration, but I have a long time before I save enough to retire.

Both short-term goals and long-term goals require you to save as much as you can whenever you can. I often hear people say they don't have enough money to save. Yet, when I hear this, I often think, "Well, in that case, you can't afford not to save." Put another way, no amount of money is too small or insignificant to save.

For example, if you save $20 a month, at the end of the year you will have $240 (more if it is in an account that draws interest). If you save $1 a day, you will have $365 at the end of the year. If you save $100 a month, you will have $1200 at the end of the year. Do you see where I'm going with this?

It doesn't matter if you are saving pennies, quarters, or dollars. The goal is to save. I began by saving spare change and depositing it into my account at the end of the year. It wasn't always fun arriving at the bank with all those pennies, but on my account statement they were transformed into beautiful dollars.

The bank tellers never turned up their noses at all those shiny coins, and neither should you.

Save whatever you are able to save. Eventually, you will be able to save more.

Now that you know why you're saving, how often, and how much, it is finally time to write down when you plan to reach your goal. A Savings Tracker (https://orderyourlife.com/collections/money/products/savings-tracker) is a great tool to help you keep track of your savings goal.

Whether you will reach your savings goal in a week, a month, 6 months, or 10 years, the important thing is to stick to your plan.

Know that you are working towards something important, and that it will take time.

2. Make Saving Automatic

Whenever possible, make saving automatic. One of the hardest things about saving is remembering to put money in your designated account, envelope, or lockbox under your bed. Where you keep your money is up to you. I used to keep the change I saved in a zip lock bag, so I'm not one to judge. However, automatic deposits have made my life much easier.

If you can make automatic deposits into your checking, savings, college fund, or retirement accounts, do it. How beautiful is it to have your work check automatically deposited into your checking account and money from your checking account automatically deposited into your savings account? That is one less thing you have to worry about during the month.

Of course, you should periodically check your accounts to make sure the automatic deposits have gone smoothly, but that is much quicker than going to the bank. In addition, you can change the deposit time schedule and amounts at any time. Set your retirement accounts up similarly.

Out of sight. Out of mind. In the bank. What's next?

3. Save More Whenever You Can

Have you gotten a raise, bonus, or tax refund? Did you need the money before you got it? Were your basic living needs being met before this amazing windfall? If so, put some (or all) of that money away.

Don't make that face at me. Save it. I know you can do it.

Since I began filing my taxes many years ago, I have always put away money if I happen to get a tax refund. No matter how large or small the refund, I usually save half of the funds and use the rest as fun money. Granted, some of my fun money became bill money when I paid extra on the principal of my car. In any case, I always save a portion of my raises and tax refunds. The extra is automatically deposited into my savings account or my retirement plan.

I guess I shouldn't complain about not having all of my fun money. After all, I was able to buy the car I wanted because of all those years I saved the extra. A car was one of my savings goals.

Bottom line – If you don't need it right now, save it. You'll need it later.

4. Don't Withdraw Your Money on a Whim

There are only two reasons to dip into your savings.

1) You have reached your savings goal. (Go forth and spend. You earned it!)

2) You have an emergency and you need the money. (Things happen. Aren't you glad you have savings?)

Aside from reaching your savings goal, you should not withdraw your money unless you have an emergency. Let's talk about what constitutes an emergency. Here is a little trivia for you. How many questions can you get right?

Q: I want the latest phone, although my current one works perfectly well. Is that an emergency?

A: NO!

Q: My car broke down and I don't have any other way to get to work. Is that an emergency?

A: Yes. If you don't go to work, you won't get paid. If you don't get paid, you can't save money.

Q: I want to buy pizza tonight, is that an emergency?

A: NO! This is a real question folks. I once had a fellow college student tell me he used his emergency money to buy pizza because he didn't feel like going to the dining hall. He bought pizza every night until he barely had any savings left. Really! Just no!

Q: My cousin (aunt, nephew, sister, brother, mother, father, spouse, friend, insert relevant relation here) called me again with another bogus emergency and needs money. I've loaned him/her money in the past and I never get it back. Is this an emergency?

A: Sadly, no, this is not an emergency.

Unfortunately, when people hear you are trying to save money, they take advantage. I have a few friends and family members to whom I would give anything. Of course, these are the kind, honest people who never ask for anything. Then, there are those scallywags who will get nothing from me. Like you, I have loaned money that has never been repaid. The solution is to stop giving away your hard-earned cash.

One way to deter freeloaders and beggars is to ask more questions than the IRS. The conversation goes something like this.

> What is the money for? Why don't you have it? Who else have you asked? How much did they give you? How many hours did you work this week? When do you get paid? How much is your check? Which bills are due this week? How much do you have left after you pay your bills? Can you give me my money back in a week? I need my money back in a week. Can you have it by Friday? Oh, you can't have it by Friday? In that case, I need daily installments of this amount for this many days. Let's write out the terms. Will you sign this contract? Oh, you don't need the money anymore? That's great. Glad I could help.

And this brings us to tip #5. Guard your money wisely.

5. Guard Your Money Wisely

To become economically savvy, you must know when to spend your money and when to hold on to it. You have worked hard to save. Encourage others to do the same. Maybe then you won't have to act like the IRS when cousin Jim comes knocking at your door. Again!

CHAPTER SEVEN

WHAT THE HECK IS
COMPOUND INTEREST?

When I began writing about becoming economically savvy, I had no intention of writing about compound interest. However, the words compound interest kept coming up.

From folks retiring and trying to figure out what to do with their money, to parents trying to save and explain why they couldn't buy a new car just yet, I couldn't get away from the question "What the heck is compound interest?"

Bottom line – Compound interest is when you earn interest on interest. The longer you allow your money to grow, the more money you will have at the end of your savings period.

Put the money you've saved in an interest-bearing account. Then, let your money work for you.

Watch my savvy YouTube video *Compound Interest Explained: A Visual Explanation Without Math* (https://youtu.be/dZcYsvruAFY) to learn more. Or read the transcript below.

Transcript

>>TYWANQUILA: Hello, everyone. If you've been following my Order Your Life Blog, you know I write about finances and becoming economically savvy.

00:08

One topic that keeps coming up is compound interest.

Instead of writing a blog about it, I've decided to create a video explaining compound interest.

Keep in mind that this is a visual explanation.

There's no math.

No formulas.

I know some of you like that.

Instead, there are a lot of beautiful visuals so you can see how your money will grow in an interest-bearing account.

00:32

Before we get started, we need to define four terms.

These terms are principal, interest, simple interest, and compound interest.

Here are the definitions.

00:47

Principal is the money you originally put into your account.

That's your starting point.

Interest is the money that a bank, or other financial institution, pays you for leaving your money in their establishment.

Yes, people will pay you to leave your money with them.

We're going to discuss two types of interest.

01:13

Simple interest and compound interest.

Simple interest is the money you earn on your principal.

In contrast, compound interest is the money you earn on

your principal and on your prior interest.

Compound interest is when you earn interest on interest.

It's called compound interest because the interest builds upon itself.

I know this sounds complicated.

So let's look at an example.

01:41

In this example, you'll be able to see the difference between simple interest and compound interest.

In this example, let's say you put $1,000 into your account at the beginning of the year.

This is your principal.

$1,000 is the money you start with, and we're going to call it principal.

02:04

The annual interest rate is 5%.

The bank will add interest to your account every month.

Therefore, interest is added monthly.

And finally, for this example, you won't add or take away any money for 12 months.

You're leaving your principal untouched for 12 months.

02:24

As a result, 12 months is your timeline.

Let's take a look at our graph and see what happens.

Here is our graph.

On the top of the graph, we have our legend.

No interest is in yellow.

Simple interest is in purple.

And compound interest is in green.

On the y-axis we have the amount of money you've earned.

Our timeline is on the x-axis.

In this case, our timeline is in months.

All right.

03:05

Now that we understand the graph, let's make some money.

03:14

For no interest, you have $1,000 at the beginning of the year and $1,000 at the end of the year. Nothing's changed.

With simple interest you have $1,000 at the beginning of the year and $1,050 at the end of the year.

Congratulations! You've earned $50.

With compound interest, you have $1,000 at the beginning of the year and $1,051.16 at the end of the year.

You earned $51.16.

03:54

That's $1,000 with no interest, $1,050 with simple interest, and $1,051.16 with compound interest.

The difference between your earnings with no interest and simple interest is $50.

The difference between your earnings with compound interest and your earnings with simple interest is $1.16.

You have earned a little more money with compound interest.

Now I know $1.16 doesn't sound like much, but there is a way for you to earn more money with compound interest.

04:42

It's time for a little Q&A for the curious.

So what will happen if you increase your timeline?

The short answer is you earn more money.

Let's see what happens when you allow your money to grow for a longer period of time.

05:02

Example 2.

So in this example, we have increased our timeline to 30 years.

That's 360 months.

As before, we'll begin with a principal of $1,000 and we will leave that money untouched for 30 years.

The annual interest rate is 5%.

Interest is added monthly.

And, as I mentioned, our new timeline – our increased timeline – is 30 years or 360 months.

Let's go to our graph.

With no interest, let's see how we do.

05:39

With no interest, you began with a thousand dollars and at the end of thirty years you still have a thousand dollars.

Surprise!

Nothing changed.

With simple interest, you have $1,000 at the beginning.

Let's go back.

06:09

There we go.

There's simple interest.

With simple interest you have $1,000 at the beginning and $2,500 after 360 months.

Let's see what we have with compound interest.

You have $1,000 at the beginning and $4,467.74 at the end of your timeline.

That's not bad for someone who started with a thousand dollars.

06:41

Let's recap.

So no interest.

You start with $1,000.

You end with $1,000.

That's an earning of zero.

With simple interest, you start with $1,000 and you end up with $2,500.

You've earned $1,500.

And finally, with compound interest, you end up with $4,467.74.

Congratulations! You have earned $3,467.74.

07:23

Here compound interest is clearly the winner.

As you can see, the longer your timeline, the more money you earn.

Well this is great.

But is there anything else that you can do to earn more interest?

What happens if you increase your principal?

07:42

Well again the short answer is you earn more money.

In our final example, we are going to see what happens when you increase your timeline and your principal.

Your principal has increased to $10,000.

Again we're leaving that $10,000 and we are not going to touch it until our timeline ends.

Annual interest rate is still 5%.

Interest added is still monthly and our timeline is still 360 months or 30 years.

Let's see what happens.

08:20

Well no interest.

You guessed it.

You start with 10,000.

You end with 10,000.

As usual, there is no change.

With simple interest, you begin with $10,000 and you end

up with $25,000.

Finally, with compound interest, you began with the same $10,000 and after 30 years you have $44,677.44.

08:54

Recap.

No interest.

Start with ten thousand.

End with ten thousand.

Zero earnings.

For simple interest, you end up with $25,000 and that means you've earned $15,000.

09:09

And finally, with compound interest, our clear winner here, you can see that the more money you put in at the beginning, the more you end up with at the end.

And in the case of compound interest, you end up with $44,677.44.

Meaning you've earned $34,677.44 over the course of your timeline.

09:33

Imagine how much you can earn if your principal is even higher or if your timeline is longer.

That is the power of compound interest.

You let your money work for you and all you have to do is wait.

09:46

Here are today's take-home messages.

Firstly, compared to no interest and simple interest, you earn more money with compound interest.

And you can clearly see that with no interest, it's not beneficial to you at all.

So either choose simple interest or, if you can, if you have that option, compound interest.

Put your money in an interest-bearing account that earns you compound interest.

10:12

To earn even more money, there are three things that you can personally do.

You can increase your timeline.

You can increase your principal.

And, ideally, you can increase your timeline and your principal.

10:27

I made this video specifically for people who want to see compound interest, but they're not necessarily interested in the math behind the magic.

So if you're one of those people who really wants to see the math, feel free to contact me.

We can talk about formulas.

We can talk about compound interest.

We can talk about simple interest and I'd be happy to talk to you.

10:49

I want to thank you all for watching my visual explanation of compound interest.

And if you have questions, feel free to email me or contact me on social media.

You can also go to OrderYourLife.com to get the latest financial tips and economically savvy advice.

Thank you!

CHAPTER EIGHT

HOW TO PAY OFF DEBT FAST, EASY, AND EARLY

Now that you understand how principal and interest work, let's reverse the situation and talk about how lenders make money. To begin, answer these three questions.

1. Are you planning to purchase a house or car?

2. Do you have a mortgage or auto loan you'd like to pay off?

3. Would you like to see your credit card debt disappear?

If you answered yes to any of these questions, I have two words for you – Principal and Interest. Yes, these are the same two terms used in the previous chapter. The difference is that lenders are collecting the interest (i.e., money flows out of your pocket and into theirs).

When it comes to debt, principal is the amount of money you borrowed from the lender. Interest is what the lender charges you for borrowing their money.

How Do Lenders Make Money?

Lenders make money by charging high interest rates, enticing you to borrow more money, and extending your lending period for as long as they can. Lenders are in the business of making money, and they are very good at it.

Let me show you how it works. Here are 5 examples.

Example 1: You have a credit card balance of $1000 (i.e., you owe the credit card company $1000). Your interest rate is 10%. Your friend also has a $1000 credit card balance. However, her interest rate is 8%.

Minimum Payment: Your credit card company calculates your minimum payment as 3% of your balance, which means that, at a minimum, you must pay $30 the first month (i.e., $1000 x .03 = $30). The credit card company recalculates your minimum payment each month. Therefore, when your balance is lower, your minimum payment is less (e.g., a $700 balance = $21 minimum payment; a $500 balance = $15 minimum payment).

The Vow: You and your friend have vowed to stop using your credit cards and pay the minimum payment each month. How long will it take each of you to pay off your credit cards? Who will pay the most interest? (Remember, as your balance goes down, so does your required minimum payment. Thus, you will be required to pay less and less on your bill each month.)

You: It will take you 71 months (i.e., 5 years and 11 months) to pay off your debt. You will pay a total of $1280.49 (the original $1000 plus $280.49 in interest).

Your Friend: It will take your friend 68 months (i.e., 5 years and 8 months) to pay off her debt. Your friend will pay a total of $1210.18 (the original $1000 plus $210.18 in interest).

The lender will make $280.49 from you and $210.18 from your friend.

Assuming another customer only pays the minimum payment on a $1000 balance, how much will the lender make on a 20% interest rate? $860.86 with 101 months (i.e., 8 years and

5 months) to pay off the debt.

24% interest rate? $1,332.19 with 125 months (i.e., 10 years and 5 months) to pay off the debt.

34% interest rate? $9,552.39 with 520 months (i.e., 43 years and 4 months) to pay off the debt.

By focusing on the small, ever-decreasing minimum payment, the lender entices you to think short-term. However, when you do the long-term math, you discover that you will be paying the lending company a lot of money for a long time.

Moreover, every time you use your credit card and only pay the minimum payment, you are prolonging your debt.

Note: Each lender has its own way of calculating your minimum payment. Some lenders use interest plus your balance, while others only use a percentage of your balance. If you are wondering how your minimum payment is calculated, most lenders disclose this information on your credit card statement, your terms of agreement, or the documents you received when you signed up for your credit card. Read the fine print. You can also contact your lender to ask how they calculate your minimum payment.

Example 2: You have a credit card balance of $1000. Your interest rate is 10%.

As in Example 1, you have vowed to stop using your credit card. This time, however, you plan to pay $30 every month, even if the required minimum payment is less than $30.

How will paying a fixed amount of $30 each month change the amount of interest you pay to the lender?

It will take you 40 months (i.e., 3 years and 4 months) to pay off your debt. You will pay a total of $1176.42 (the original

$1000 plus $176.42 in interest). When compared to only paying the minimum payment, you will save yourself 2 years and 7 months and $104.07 in interest. (Reminder: If you only pay the minimum payment, it will take you 5 years and 11 months to pay off your debt plus $280.49 in interest).

If you pay $50 each month, it will take you 22 months (i.e., 1 year and 10 months) to pay off your debt. You will pay a total of $1098.49 (the original $1000 plus $98.49 in interest).

If you pay $100 each month, it will take you 11 months to pay off your debt. You will pay a total of $1048.58 (the original $1000 plus $48.58 in interest).

By paying more than the minimum payment each month, you reduce your lending period. A short lending period means you will pay less interest to the lender.

Note: Having a low credit card balance improves your credit utilization rate (also called a credit utilization ratio). Utilization rate is your total credit balance divided by your total available credit. Lenders use utilization rate to determine if you are a credit risk. A high utilization rate may also indicate that you are in financial distress.

Note: If you pay your credit card balance in full every month, you will not pay any interest. If your credit card offers rewards or cash back, you will still earn rewards for your purchases, even if you pay your bill in full each month.

Note: If you pay your credit card bill on time and you do not go over your credit limit, contact your lender to request a lower interest rate. They may be able to review your account and lower your rate. If the lender cannot lower your rate, ask what you can do to possibly get a lower rate in the future.

Example 3: You want to buy a house. You assess your income and expenses and decide what you can afford. You set your budget at $150,000. When you apply for a mortgage loan, you discover that you are preapproved for $300,000.

What do you do? Do you purchase a bigger, more expensive house?

Let's assume that, no matter the cost of the house, your interest rate will be 6% and you will have a 30-year mortgage.

If you purchase the $150,000 house, your monthly payment will be $899.33. Over 30 years, you will pay a total of $323,754.57 (the original $150,000 plus $173,754.57 in interest).

If you purchase the $300,000 house, your monthly payment will be $1,798.65. Over 30 years, you will pay $647,515.59 (the original $300,000 plus $347,515.59 in interest).

When you buy a more expensive house, you pay more interest and the lender makes more money.

In addition to the cost of the house, monthly payments are another factor to consider (see the next example).

Note: When you buy a more expensive house, the realtor may receive a higher commission, which means more money in his or her pocket. Find a good realtor who will look out for your best interests. Most realtors are honest and will do everything they can to help you find a good home. However, there are realtors who will pressure you to buy the most expensive house on the market, even if you can't afford it.

Note: Your interest rate will likely vary with the cost of your house. For this example, the same interest rate was chosen to simplify the calculations and focus exclusively on the comparison of a less expensive vs. more expensive house. However, in reality, your mortgage lender will use your credit history, asset value, the price of the house, debt-to-income ratio, and other financial factors to determine your interest rate. Some lenders may even offer a lower interest rate for a less expensive house.

Example 4: You have decided to purchase a $200,000 house. This is higher than your budget, but lower than the preapproved amount. You have the option of 1) getting a 15-year loan with an interest rate of 6% and a monthly payment of $1,687.71 or 2) getting a 30-year loan with an interest rate of 6% and a monthly payment of $1,199.10. Do you choose the loan with fewer years or the loan with the lower monthly payment?

For the 15-year loan, you will pay a total of $303,788.86 (the original $200,000 plus $103,788.86 in interest).

For the 30-year loan, you will pay a total of $431,677.05 (the original $200,000 plus $231,677.05 in interest).

In this scenario, you must decide if you prefer to pay less in interest or if you want a lower monthly payment.

Note: Although a 15-year mortgage would likely have a lower interest rate, for simplicity's sake, in this example, both loan terms have an interest rate of 6%. When you talk to potential mortgage lenders, ask them about interest rates for different scenarios (e.g., cost of the home, length of the mortgage, percent of the down payment). Although they may be a little annoyed with you, most lenders will calculate – and recalculate – monthly payments and interest rates for varying scenarios. Write down the calculations, compare them, and make the decision that works best for you and your family.

Example 5: You have decided to purchase a $20,000 car. You have saved $5,000 for a down payment on the car. When you arrive at the dealership, the salesperson tells you they are running a special for zero down payment, and you qualify.

The auto loan has a 5% interest rate, 72-month loan term, and you are not trading in a vehicle. Do you choose to pay the down payment or not?

With no down payment, you pay $322.10 a month. Over the course of the loan, you will pay a total of $23,191.14 (the original $20,000 plus $3,191.14 in interest).

With a $5,000 down payment, you pay $241.57 a month. Over the course of the loan, you will pay a total of $22,393.33 (the original $20,000 plus $2,393.33 in interest).

Note: If you increase or decrease the amount of your down payment, your monthly payment and loan term may change.

Note: This example does not include taxes or fees, which vary by location. Before purchasing a vehicle, research the taxes and fees in your area. Find out how they will affect your loan or monthly payment.

Note: Have you ever wondered why car salespeople ask what you want your monthly payment to be? Primarily, they ask because they want you to focus on the smaller number of the monthly payment instead of the larger number of the total price of the car plus interest. Secondly, they ask because by extending your loan term to 60 months or 72 months or 84 months, they can offer you a lower monthly payment. However, remember that a longer loan term means they will make more money off of you. Also keep in mind that 60, 72, and 84 months translate into 5, 6, and 7 years of car payments. I told you lenders were smart. They do their best to get you to focus on smaller numbers and think in months instead of years. Before going to a car dealership, know what you want to pay. Do the math.

Pay Off Debt Fast

The fastest way to pay off debt is to pay on the principal.

When you pay on a loan or credit card, the first part of the payment goes toward interest. Yes, the lenders get their money first. Whatever is left over goes toward your remaining principal.

For example, you just purchased a $20,000 car with a 5% interest rate, 72-month loan term, and no down payment. Your monthly car note is $322.10. When you pay your first bill, $83.33 goes to the interest and $238.77 goes to the principal. After paying your bill, you still owe $19,761.23.

Similarly, you purchased a $200,000 house with a 6% interest rate, 30-year loan term, and no down payment. Your monthly mortgage payment is $1,199.10. When you pay your first bill, $1,000 goes to the interest and $199.10 goes to the principal. After paying your bill, you still owe $199,800.90.

As you can see, those initial monthly payments do not go far. Moreover, this process happens every month, which is why it takes years to pay off debt. Sadly, by the time you finish paying for your purchases, your car may be falling apart and your house may be in need of repair. The car salesperson will welcome you back with a smile, and the bank will be ready to offer you a home equity loan or the option to refinance. It's time for the lender to make more money.

Note: Depending on your situation, refinancing your mortgage or getting a home equity loan can be good financial options. Research your options and decide what is right for you.

Let's Talk About Principal

In contrast to paying the exact amount that is listed on your bill each month, if you put extra funds towards the principal, you will pay off your debt faster.

For instance, on your $20,000 auto loan, pay the required monthly payment plus put an additional $100 toward the principal every month.

You will save $864.82 in interest and pay off your car loan 19 months early (i.e., 1 year and 7 months early).

Paying extra on the principal decreases your loan amount. The same concept applies to mortgages and credit cards.

For credit cards, paying additional money is called an extra payment (not principal). However, the bottom line is that by paying more than the minimum payment, you will pay off your credit card debt faster and pay less interest.

Pay Off Debt Easily

The easiest way to pay off debt is to make principal payments automatic. Some lenders make it easy for you. They will automatically deduct your regular payment and your principal payments from your account. All you have to do is set up the process.

Some lenders make the process moderately difficult. You have to check a box or enter a specific amount for the principal each time you make a payment.

Some lenders make it extremely difficult for you to make principal payments. First, you have to figure out how and where to send the principal payments, because their regular payment system is separate from their principal payment system. Then, you have to write a check and mail the principal payment because there is not an online or automatic system.

If you are working with a lender who makes it difficult to make principal payments, take heart. Remember, their goal is to make as much money as possible and your goal is to pay as little interest as possible. Think of it as a little competition – one that you will win.

Make the process easier for yourself by printing cheap or homemade address labels so you don't have to constantly write the lender's name on envelopes. If possible, print the address directly on the envelopes and have them ready for mailing future payments.

If the lender requires you to send a letter with each principal payment, type the letter, print a dozen copies, and sign and date the letter before you mail it.

Do whatever you have to do to make those principal payments.

Pay Off Debt Early

When would you like to pay off your debt?

To pay off your debt early, think about how much extra money you need to put towards the principal of your loan. The more money you contribute to the principal, the earlier you will pay off your debt.

To find out how fast you can pay off your debt, use a loan calculator. There are dozens of calculators out there. Here are a few that are easy to use.

Credit Card Calculators

Bankrate

Credit Karma

SmartAsset

Experian

Mortgage Calculators

Dave Ramsey

Bankrate

The Mortgage Reports

Car Loan Calculators

Calculator.net

Bankrate

NerdWallet

General Debt Calculators

Calculator.net - Debt Payoff

Calculator.net - Amortization

Credit Karma - Amortization

YouCanDealWithIt.com - Debt Repayment

In Closing

In addition to knowing how to pay off your debt, there are a few things to remember. Make sure you pay on the principal, watch out for penalties, request a detailed statement, request an amortization schedule, and do the math.

1. Pay on the principal. Adding extra money to your bill payment is not the same as paying on the principal. Extra payments are usually applied to the next month's interest. Although some lenders may apply a small portion of your extra payment to the principal, generally, the entirety of extra payments do not go directly to the principal. You must specify, either in writing or by selecting a specific section on an online payment system, how you want the lender to apply your payment. When in doubt, ask your lender to clarify the process. Always verify that your

principal payments are indeed going towards the principal.

2. Watch out for penalties. Check to make sure there are not any penalties for paying off your debt early. Some lenders charge fees for early payment. If there is a fee, do the math to determine what is most beneficial for you – sticking to the lender's payment schedule or paying off your debt early by paying the fee.

3. Request a detailed statement. Does your lender provide you with a detailed statement showing all of the payments you have made since the inception of the loan? If so, your lender may send the statement in the mail, or it may be available through your online account. If not, ask your lender for a detailed billing statement showing all payments, including how your payments were split between principal and interest.

4. Request an amortization schedule (also called an amortization table). Amortization is the act of paying off debt in equal installments over a specific period of time. Although amortization tables are usually associated with mortgages, an amortization schedule can be generated for any type of loan. An amortization schedule is simply a table that shows the loan amount, loan term (e.g., 30 years, 72 months), payment period (e.g., monthly, quarterly, yearly), and how much of each payment goes towards interest and principal.

With mortgages and car loans, initially, a small portion of the payment goes towards principal. Over time, more of the funds go towards principal and the amount going to interest gradually decreases.

Your lender may send you an amortization schedule, or it may be available via your online account. If your lender does not provide access to an amortization schedule, you can create your own using an online calculator (e.g., Calculator.net or

Credit Karma).

5. Do the math. When considering multiple strategies for paying off your debt, do the math first. Consider all of your options and decide which loan terms are best for you. Don't let the lenders have all the fun. You are in control of your finances. Pay off your debt on your own terms.

With discipline and planning, you can pay off your debt faster, easier, and earlier. Simply remember these two words – principal and interest.

CHAPTER NINE

50 WAYS TO PAY FOR COLLEGE
AND GRADUATE SCHOOL

Did you know you don't have to pay for college?

Sure, you have to pay for tuition, room, board, and books. But that money does not have to come out of your pocket.

If you take the time to plan for college, you can graduate debt free, or very nearly so. To do this, you will need tenacity and foresight. You will need to put in a lot of hours doing research. You will need to work hard to ensure you have very little debt when you graduate.

Don't tell me it's impossible. Don't tell me I'm dreaming.

I am the reality. I went to college debt free.

My friends joked that I was being paid to go to college. It was true. I always received a refund at the end of the semester. My scholarships totaled more than my tuition.

What my friends didn't joke about was the fact that I began researching scholarships in high school. They didn't joke about the fact that I worked all through college. They didn't joke about the fact that I knew my family couldn't afford to pay for college. They didn't joke about the fact that I had to plan for college, because I knew I would have limited options if I failed to plan.

Disclaimer: I took out a loan one summer to study abroad. I paid that loan back in full while I was in graduate school. I also paid off my car.

No, I didn't pay for graduate school either. Yes, I worked all through graduate school. Yes, I was debt free when I received my Ph.D.

How did I do it? With hard work, planning, researching, and applying to every scholarship I was even halfway qualified for. I also maintained good grades, and studied hard for standardized tests. I set target scores for the PSAT, ACT, SAT, and GRE. Then, I studied every day and did my best to achieve those targets.

There are scholarships, grants, and fellowships for every kind of student, for every individual from every walk of life. There are funds for students who have jobs, good grades, high test scores, solid records of community service, a parent in the military, have been in foster care, or experienced other hardships in their lives. There are scholarships for artists and musicians, poets and dancers, gamers and aspiring farmers. There are even scholarships for people who can trace their ancestry to another country or an historical event.

You don't have to pay for college or graduate school. You can graduate debt free. Let me show you how.

50+ Funding Opportunities

Here are more than 50 opportunities that will help you fund your education. There are thousands more out there. This is just a taste of the funds available to you.

Ancestry

American Indian Graduate Center

Amish Descendant Scholarship Fund

APIA Scholars

Cobell Scholarship

TheDream.US

The Gates Scholarship

Hispanic Scholarship Fund

The Jackie Robinson Foundation

Ron Brown Scholar Program

UNCF

Arts and Entertainment

Crossword Hobbyist

Doodle for Google

Floyd Mayweather Jr. Foundation

The Gallery Collection

Gamers Helping Gamers

Helen McCloy Scholarships

House of Blues Music Forward Foundation

Student Academy Awards

Easy and Odd

Debt.com

DoSomething.org

Foreclosure.com

Niche

Toyota TeenDrive365

Unigo

Graduate School

Institute for Humane Studies

Jacob K. Javits Fellowships Program

Josephine de Karman Fellowship

NIH Fellowships

NSF Graduate Research Fellowship

Spencer Foundation

Jobs and Employers

Most major employers offer scholarships and tuition assistance programs to their employees. If you are currently working, find out how you can quality for your company's program. If you are not currently working, research employers in your area and find out what they have to offer. Then get a job at one of these employers, and work towards qualifying for their scholarships.

Languages and Linguistics

BRIC Language Systems

Critical Language Scholarship Program

Life Events

American Cancer Society

Cancer for College

Foster Care to Success

Horatio Alger Association

Jack Kent Cooke Foundation

Jeannette Rankin Women's Scholarship Fund

National Collegiate Cancer Foundation

National Foster Parent Association

Merit Scholarships

Coca-Cola Scholars Foundation

PSAT/NMSQT - National Merit Scholarship Program

Military and Armed Services

American Legion Auxiliary

Children of Fallen Patriots

Marine Corps Scholarship Foundation

Purple Heart Foundation

Scholarship Directories

There are dozens of great scholarship directories. Most of these directories have been compiled over years, and they are excellent sources for little known scholarships and grants.

AAUW

American Association of Cosmetology Schools

Discover

Lead with Languages

Scholarship America

Scholarships.com

Society of Women Engineers

Trade School Future

UNCF

Unigo

Hidden Opportunities

Most colleges and universities have special scholarships and funds that are only available to their students. The scholarships may be offered by major, financial need, GPA, or year in school. As you research colleges, talk to people in the financial aid office, the department head for the major you're interested in, current and former students, and current professors. You'll be surprised at the small grants, funding opportunities, and jobs available at your university. To learn about them, all you have to do is ask.

States, counties, and towns also have scholarships they only offer to local residents. Contact your city hall, chamber of commerce, local businesses, school counselor, and community service organizations to find out about local scholarships and grants. Search online to learn about opportunities in your state.

Work for It

In addition to the opportunities above, search for part-time and on-campus jobs. Jobs in libraries, computer labs, museums, and theaters allow you to earn extra money (and potentially complete your school work while on the job). Jobs in cafeterias, restaurants, markets, and stores allow you to make money (and potentially get discounts on anything you buy).

While in college and graduate school, I worked a number of jobs during the school year and summer. I consciously chose jobs and internships that offered perks or helped build my resume. For example, I worked in the cafeteria (free meal plan plus a paycheck), the library (study time and access to free course materials), as a graduate assistant (good pay and a leadership role), and a research assistant (hard work and resume builder that likely helped me get into graduate school).

You Don't Have to Pay for College

Although there are no free and easy roads to higher education, it is possible to minimize your debt. If you don't want to spend a fortune on college or graduate school, you have to work hard before you walk across the graduation stage.

I've shared more than 50 options to help you pay for your education. You can do this. There is money waiting for you.

You don't have to pay for college, unless you want to.

CHAPTER TEN

7 STEPS TO RETIREMENT PLANNING

Retirement planning requires a long-term approach and discipline. Although the objective is simple, the process is complicated.

The Objective: amass enough funds and assets to live comfortably in retirement

The Process: plan before retirement, stick to the plan pre- and post-retirement, effectively execute the plan during retirement

Planning for retirement begins with thinking about your retirement goals. Ask yourself these retirement questions.

Retirement Questions

- At what age would you like to retire?

- Where would you like to live?

- What activities or hobbies would you like to pursue?

- How much money will you need monthly, or annually, to live the life you want to live?

- Do you have debt (e.g., credit cards, mortgage, student loans) and will you carry that debt into retirement?

- Will you retire with a spouse or partner? (If yes, involve them in the planning process.)

- Will you care for dependents (e.g., children,

grandchildren, or parents) during retirement?

- What healthcare expenses do you expect to have during retirement?

- Based on life expectancy and heath factors, how long can you expect to be in retirement? (This question sounds morbid but, depending on the age at which you retire and your health status, you may spend 20 or 30+ years in retirement.)

- How long do you have to meet your financial retirement goals? (The answer to this question will determine whether you need to accelerate your planning process and savings goals.)

You may not have all the answers right now. Yet, no matter your age, you should start visualizing your ideal retirement life.

After thinking about the questions above (and hopefully answering some of them), you are ready to begin the seven steps of retirement planning.

1. Start Now

Whether you are decades from retirement or a few years from retirement, now is the best time to start saving and planning. If you want those decades of retirement to be relaxing and enjoyable, the last thing you want to stress about is money.

Younger planners have the advantage of time on their side. They can take advantage of compound interest and make riskier investments.

Older planners have the advantage of knowledge and experience on their side. They can better visualize their retirement futures, answer retirement questions, and verbalize their retirement goals.

Whether you are a younger planner or an older planner, a plan is essential to charting your retirement course. If you don't save and plan for retirement, you may have to work longer than you want. While in retirement, one financial emergency may put you in debt or force you to downsize to make ends meet.

If you don't plan, you are at risk of foregoing your retirement dreams and living a life you don't want to live.

2. Participate in Your Employer's Matching Program

If you are fortunate enough to have an employer who matches your retirement contributions, participate in the program to the maximum extent possible. For example, if an employer matches up to 5% of your contribution, contribute 5%.

If you contribute 2%, your employer will match your 2%. But why settle for 2% when you can have 5%?

I've heard people say they can't afford to participate in matching. The reality is you can't afford not to participate. Can you name another time when your employer will give you money because you are investing in yourself and your future?

Once you are vested (i.e., you have worked for the company for a specified amount of time and you are eligible to keep all of your employer's contributions without penalty), that money is yours. If you leave the company, you can take your contributions and your employer's contributions with you. That's a win-win situation (for you anyway).

It is your responsibility to plan for your retirement, not your employer's. Take advantage of matching.

Note: Check with your employer to find out when you will become vested. Vesting periods vary by company. At some companies, employees are vested on the first day of employment.

At other companies, employees are vested after a few years.

3. Steadily Increase Your Contributions

If you are not able to contribute the full matching percentage or amount, steadily increase your contributions every year, every quarter, or whenever you get a raise or bonus.

If you are able to contribute the full matching percentage or amount, the same rule applies – continually increase your contributions.

Your employer may even have a system in place whereby your contributions will automatically increase by 1% every year until you reach a specific contribution percentage. Find out if your employer offers automatic increases and ask how you can activate the process. An automatic process will make it easier for you to increase your contributions and reach your financial retirement goals.

Steadily increase your retirement contributions until you have maxed out what you can afford to contribute or until you reach the maximum contribution amount allowed by law. (Yes, there are limits and they vary from year to year. https://www.irs.gov/retirement-plans/plan-participant-employee/retirement-topics-contributions)

4. Contribute as Much as You Can

Notice I did not say increase your contributions until you reach the maximum percentage your company will match. Instead, increase your contributions until you are putting as much money towards retirement as you can afford.

Can you afford to contribute 6%? 8%? 10%? If you can, do it. The interest on your investment should compound and grow as the length of time you are invested increases.

What happens if you can't sustain the contribution percentage or you have a life event that requires you to use those funds for something else? That's easy. Decrease your retirement contributions.

Contribution percentages aren't set in stone. You can move them up and down as needed. Check with your employer to find out if there are restrictions on when or how often you can adjust your contributions. Also ask how long it takes contribution changes to go into effect.

Contributing as much as you can, when you can, will set you on the path to a more comfortable retirement. You do not have to forsake all leisure and recreation in the present in preparation for your retirement in the future. However, by building your nest egg now, you will create a cushion for those times when you are not able to contribute as much towards retirement.

5. Determine How Much You'll Need to Live Comfortably

Are you looking forward to traveling the world when you retire? Or are you planning to spend long, tranquil days fishing at the lake near your home? Your activities during retirement will determine how much money you will need to live comfortably.

Depending on your retirement goals, you may need a lot of money, or you may need very little money. For example, travelers and explorers, do you plan to travel first class and stay at 5-star hotels? Or will you take your fully paid for RV on a trip that never ends? For fishing fans and nature lovers, will you need new equipment and gear every year? Or will your old equipment do just fine?

Write down possible expenses you will incur during retirement. Create a financial plan that accounts for housing, medical care, insurance, food, utilities, leisure activities, emergency funds, cost of living increases, and any other expected expenses.

Use your financial plan as the basis for estimating your living expenses. This estimate will help you determine how much you need to save for retirement, and how much you will need to withdraw from your investments during retirement.

Before retirement, review your plan at least once a year to ensure you are not missing important expense categories. During retirement, review your plan at least twice a year, or as your situation and needs change.

6. Pay Off All Debt

Before you hit the I'm officially retired button, pay off all of your debt. When you retire, your income will likely decrease. Even if you plan to receive an annuity, social security, or other types of income during retirement, your post-retirement incoming funds probably won't total 100% of your pre-retirement incoming funds. Furthermore, depending on the state where you retire, you may have to pay taxes on your retirement income.

In preparation for a decreased income, pay off your mortgage, auto loans, student loans, consumer loans, credit cards, and other longstanding or recurring debt. You may be excited about retiring, but your lenders won't be concerned about your new status. They will want their money, and you are honor-bound to pay it.

If you decide to retire before paying off your debt, contact your lenders before you retire. Ask them about payment plans and reduced payment options. Most lenders will be willing to work with you to ensure you can still pay your bills on time.

If you do pay off your debt, put your extra monthly funds

(i.e., the money you would have spent on bills) in an interest-bearing account, an emergency fund, or a fun fund that you can dip into during retirement. If you have extra funds on hand during retirement, you will be able to live more comfortably and worry-free. Additionally, if there is an emergency, you will have cash reserves, and you may not have to use your retirement funds to cover an emergency situation.

7. Call Around and Ask Questions

Talk to people from different financial agencies and institutions, even if you don't plan to invest your retirement funds with them. Learn what they have to say. Ask them to send you retirement information. Prepare a list of questions and compare their answers.

Yes, you can call and ask questions without making a commitment. After your conversation, you may decide to invest with that company. Or you may decide that company is not right for you. In either case, the goal is to learn as much as you can, which will enable you to make the right decision for yourself.

During your calls, remember that the agent's job is to get you to open an account. Do not let them pressure you into making a decision on the spot. At the beginning of the conversation, let them know you are calling to learn and get more information. Be honest and tell them you are not yet ready to make a commitment. Start your inquires by stating that your goal is to learn; most agents will be kind, courteous, and willing to answer your questions.

In addition to calling companies, participate in multiple retirement planning meetings, seminars, and webinars. These meetings may be hosted by your employer, someone else's employer, or offered by a retirement or investment company.

Many employers and investment companies offer seminars and webinars that are open to the public. Some even post online videos and transcripts from their meetings. If you are not able to attend a meeting in person, search online for free content. There are a lot of good videos and webinars available from reputable companies.

I have learned a lot by attending retirement sessions and webinars. Each time I attend one, I learn something new (or am reminded of something I have forgotten). The more I learn about preparing for retirement, the more I want to know. Plus, most presenters are happy to share their knowledge; they appreciate good questions and will do everything they can to make sure your questions are answered.

Bonus

Watch out for the temptation to withdraw your retirement funds early. There are consequences associated with early withdrawals. There are fees, taxes, and early withdrawal penalties. Before withdrawing your funds, consider all of your options and do the math.

What percentage of your funds will go towards fees? Is it worth withdrawing the money before you meet the withdrawal requirements? If you have retirement savings at a previous job, can you do a rollover instead of a withdrawal? (Definitions: With a withdrawal, you remove the money from your retirement plan, which may incur penalties or fees. With a rollover, you move the money from one type of retirement program to another type of retirement program, which usually does not incur penalties or fees.)

Talk to a professional (or multiple professionals) to determine the consequences of early withdrawals and whether the option is right for you. Determine if you should do a rollover instead.

Choices

There are people who *want* to work until they are 80. Good on them for staying active!

In contrast, there are people who *have* to work until they are 80. I wonder what they would have done differently, if they could turn back the clock.

When you retire should be a choice, not a struggle to hold on for a few more years until you can afford to retire.

Is retirement a choice for you or is it a chore? If it is the latter, what will you do to expand your choices, retire when you choose, and ensure you live your best life?

PART II:
MONEY MATTERS FOR KIDS

CHAPTER ELEVEN

6 WAYS TO TEACH YOUR CHILDREN
ABOUT MONEY

When was the last time you talked to your kids about money? What do they know about earning, spending, saving, and investing?

If you have not talked to your children about money, or explained to them the concepts of earning money, managing money, or paying a myriad of bills with your money, they may think you have an unlimited quantity of financial resources.

Money does not grow on trees. It does not magically fall out of an ATM. It does not appear in your account like magic fairy dust every time you need more of it.

It is an asset that can take years to earn and seconds to lose.

Money misconceptions arise partly from the fact that many money transactions are digital (e.g., direct deposit, auto bill pay, credit and debit cards).

Misconceptions also arise because families don't talk about money. Even teenagers may find it hard to understand why you can't buy them everything they want.

Most primary and secondary schools don't teach financial literacy.

Banks don't offer you a money management class when you make your first deposit.

Employers may provide workshops about retirement investments, but these workshops are usually optional, and most people work years before they attend one.

Given all of these challenges, name three ways you expect your child to learn about money.

Who is in the best position to teach your children? You guessed it. You.

Give your children the gift of knowledge. Teach them what they need to know.

Tips for Teaching Your Children About Money

1. Put Money in Clear Jars

Use clear jars of different sizes to teach your child about quantity, time, and goals.

Quantity

Ask your child how many coins it would take to fill up each jar. Fill each jar and write down how many coins fit it the jar.

If your child is learning to count, you can use one coin denomination (e.g., only put pennies in the jars). Then, count the number of coins in each jar.

If your child is older, use different coin denominations. Then, count the total amount of money in each jar.

The goal is to show your child that bigger jars require more coins.

Time

Set a timer to discover how long it takes to fill each jar. Set the timer. Fill one jar. Then write down the amount of time it took to fill the jar.

Keep setting the timer and filling the jars until you have written down all the times. Which jar did your child fill the fastest?

You can turn your jar filling task into a race to see who can fill each jar the quickest.

For a fast, frantically fun race, put coins in the jar by the handful; there is no limit on how many coins can go in the jar at the same time.

For a slower, steadier race, set a rule that racers can only put one coin in the jar at a time. For an additional challenge, add that anyone who puts more than one coin in the jar at a time has to empty their jar and start over.

You may want to designate someone as the money referee for your races.

Whether your race is fast or slow, the goal is to show your child that bigger jars take longer to fill.

Goals

Quantity and time are great ways to teach your children about savings goals. It takes more money and more time to save for a bigger goal.

Consider turning your clear jars into savings jars. Each jar can represent a different savings goal. Small goals have little jars and big goals have large jars.

How long will it take to reach the smallest goal? How long will it take to reach the biggest goal?

Write your child's goal on each jar, or put a picture of the desired item on the jar.

2. Make It a Game

If you want to mix things up, turn your clear jar money activity into a game. Before counting the coins, ask your child to guess the number of coins or the amount of money that is in each jar.

Offer a prize for the right answer or the closest answer. The prize could be the money in the jar, a percentage of the money in the jar, or another amount of money based on how close your child's answer is to the right answer.

Have fun with the game. Add dollar bills to the jar, ask other family members to make guesses, or contribute the winning prize money to your child's savings account or savings goal.

You can even let them put the money in the jars and have you guess the amounts. What fun prize can you get for guessing the right answer?

Get creative and make the money jar game fun for your child.

3. Create a Visual Timeline

Make money visual for your child. Create a money timeline or design a money calendar.

Each time your child has a money event (e.g., receives money), write a note on the timeline or calendar.

Use stickers and drawings to add color and visual interest to your money work of art.

If you are creating a timeline, use strips of paper for each money event that happens in your child's life. As you add events, tape the strips of paper together and fold them like an accordion. At the end of each month, the end of the year, or when your child has reached a savings milestone, unfold the strips of paper and discuss the money timeline with your child.

To add dimensionality to your timeline, use narrow strips of paper for small money events and wide strips of paper for large events. Encourage your child to use different colors of paper and different types of stickers for each money event.

The visual timeline serves as a way to help your child track financial goals. It also makes your child's money events visible, which reinforces the principles of quantity, time, and goals.

4. Take Your Child Shopping With You

To be clear, taking your child shopping with you really means take them shopping and let them spend their own money. Show them that the things they want and need are not free.

Physically going to a store and handing a cashier their money will make the concepts of spending, saving, and earning more real.

Before going to the store, take a picture of your child's clear money jar. Let your child take some money out of the jar. Write down the amount of the deduction. Then, take another picture of the jar. The pictures serve as visual records of deducting money from the jar.

For younger children, you may want to add the pictures to their money timeline. Even if they aren't great at counting yet, younger children will be able to tell you that there is less money in the jar.

For older children, consider keeping a ledger (i.e., balance sheet) of how much money they add and deduct from the jars. Use the ledger to mimic keeping track of an account balance at a bank.

If your child has a bank account, debit card, or savings account, have them check their account balance before they make the purchase. Ask them to check their balance again after they make the purchase.

By shopping with your child, and letting them spend their own money, you are teaching them about debits and balances.

You are also teaching them how to manage their money in real time.

5. Do Math While You Shop

While shopping in the store, or browsing online, do math with your child.

If they want a new toy or a pair of shoes, ask them how much money they have, how long it took to save the money, how long it would take to afford the item they want, and how long it would take them to refill their jar or account after they buy their toy or shoes.

If your child decides to buy the item, that's fine. If they decide not to buy the item, that's fine too.

The point of this exercise is not to discourage your child from buying the item they want. The goal is to help them think about money and money management.

As an additional benefit of doing the math and asking questions, you and your child will become more comfortable talking to each other about money.

The money math discussion encourages you and your child to ask important money questions.

It also lets your child know it is necessary to think about what they want, reflect on their spending habits, and plan for how they will reach their financial goals.

6. Talk About Needs vs Wants

Now that you and your child have discussed money and enjoyed some money racing games, it is time to talk about needs versus wants.

Explain to your child that there are things they need to survive (e.g., food, water, shelter) and things that they want but do not need to survive (e.g., video games, toys, expensive clothes).

For younger children, start simply. Ask them about items around the house. Ask if it each item is something your family needs or something your family wants. Start with obvious things.

For example, does your child need 10 dolls or 20 toy trucks? Do they need the breakfast you made this morning? Don't be surprised if your child says they need at least some of those toys.

If talking about your child's belongings doesn't encourage them to distinguish between needs vs wants, ask them about something you or your family owns.

For example, does your family need 20 place settings for a family of 4? Do you need 6 winter coats? Does your family need a house to live in?

Keep asking questions and providing explanations until your child understands needs vs wants.

For older children, let them help you make decisions about what to buy based on your budget, your family's needs, and your family's wants.

Ask them if your family really needs the item. Then ask if there is a way to get that item at a discount or on sale.

Let your child know that it is okay to get what they want, but first, they have to get what they need.

Distinguishing between needs and wants is a money management strategy. Teach your children to prioritize their needs over their wants.

Developing healthy financial habits takes time. Set your children on the right path by teaching them about money.

Provide your children with the tools they need to build a healthy financial future.

CHAPTER TWELVE

9 EDUCATIONAL MONEY GAMES
YOUR CHILD WILL LOVE

How do the words "let's learn to manage your money" make you feel?

You likely had one of four reactions.

One, you became super excited and can't wait to get started.

Two, your heart rate remained normal and your neutral reaction is sure, why not.

Three, you cringed and feelings of dread caused goosebumps to appear all over your body.

Four, you went into total avoidance mode and pretended you never saw those words.

If you are super excited or neutral, you are going to love today's lesson.

If you are cringing or pretending the words money management do not exist, fear not. Today's money management lesson is going to be fun.

Financial education doesn't have to be boring.

There are entertaining games that will bring everyone together for family game night, while simultaneously teaching your children about financial responsibility.

Without mentioning the words learning, management, or money, you and your children can get excited about investments, budgets, and economics.

These educational lessons have been cleverly disguised as games.

You and your child will have fun learning about money.

Sneaky secret – financial education games aren't just for children. They are also for adults and the kid in you.

9 Financial Literacy Board Games, Video Games, and Card Games

1. Monopoly

Game Type: Board, Video

Monopoly is a classic board game that will teach your children the value of real estate. Your children will buy property, sell property, build their assets, and have their plans changed with the flip of a chance card.

There are also themed, video game, and junior versions of Monopoly.

2. Animal Crossing: New Horizons

Game Type: Video

Animal Crossing is a video game in which economics lessons are cleverly disguised as gameplay. Your children will learn to pay their mortgage, invest in the stalk market, and build infrastructure to improve and sustain life on the island.

3. The Allowance Game

Game Type: Board

The Allowance Game is board game in which children must do chores to earn an allowance. Your children will learn to make change, save money, and manage money.

4. Stardew Valley

Game Type: Video, Board

Stardew Valley is a multiplayer, cooperative video game. Your children will learn to work with others, build a farm, and manage money.

Stardew Valley has also been adapted into a board game.

5. Cashflow for Kids

Game Type: Board

Cashflow for Kids was created by the author of Rich Dad, Poor Dad. The board game focuses on getting out of the rat race. Your children will learn about assets, liabilities, and financial decision making.

There is also a version of Cashflow for adults and older children.

6. Net Worth

Game Type: Card

Net Worth is a card game that requires strategy and critical thinking. Your children will learn about assets, liabilities, net worth, and how to protect their assets from financial crises.

7. Catan

Game Type: Board, Card, Dice

Catan is a board game that takes you back in time. Your children will learn to trade, barter, and manage their resources.

There are many themed versions of Catan as well as card and dice games.

8. Civilization

Game Type: Video, Board

Civilization is a series of strategy video games in which players gather resources, trade, and build alliances. Your children will learn to manage resources, negotiate, and build an empire.

There is also a board game based on the video game series.

9. Minecraft

Game Type: Video, Board, App

Minecraft is a video game with an infinitely expanding 3D world. Your children will learn to gather resources, exchange goods, build structures, and explore the laws of supply and demand.

There is also a Minecraft board game and an app.

Learn to Manage Your Money

After reading about all of the fun games you and your children can play, how do the words "let's learn to manage your money" make you feel?

Get your children excited about money management.

Create new memories of family fun as you play these games together.

Offer your children a head start. Give them fun gaming lessons in money management.

CHAPTER THIRTEEN

5 TIPS TO TEACH TEENAGERS ABOUT FINANCIAL RESPONSIBILITY

Teenagers are in the unenviable position of being almost grown, but not old enough to do whatever they want.

No matter how much they test your nerves, push the boundaries, or make you wonder when an alien replaced your sweet little darling, your teenager is still a child who needs guidance.

While you can't always control who their friends are or be with them 24/7, you can offer them financial advice that will put them on the right path to being financially responsible.

If you're wondering "How can I tell my kid what to do with money when I'm so bad at controlling my own financial future?" take heart. Becoming financially responsible is a learning process. You and your teen can learn together.

Be a role model. Teach your kids about being fiscally responsible.

You can't predict the future, but one day your child may be financially responsible for you.

5 Fiscal Tips for Teenagers

1. Teach Your Teen the Value of Work

If possible, allow your teenager to get a job. Working for pay gives your teen opportunities to earn money, manage money, and learn to be responsible. Additionally, they will have your support and guidance while they learn life's lessons.

If your teen is unable to find a job at a store, restaurant, or other establishment, or they are not of legal age to work, there are alternatives. For example, your teenager can earn money by working for neighbors or family friends (e.g., mowing lawns, doing chores, tutoring, babysitting).

If you decide to pay your teen for doing work around your house, only pay them for doing extra work. Anything that is part of their regular household chores does not merit extra pay (e.g., making their bed is not a pay-worthy activity; it is something they should already be doing).

Teach your child that when they work, they get paid. When they don't work, they don't get paid.

Have you ever heard the saying "If you don't work, you don't eat?" Although you may still be able to provide some measure of support to your family, if you don't work, your child doesn't eat as often, as well, or as healthily as you would like.

Explain to your teen that you earn money to provide food and shelter for yourself and your family. Eventually, they will have similar responsibilities.

Let your child know that working hard isn't only about money. Being able to provide for oneself increases self-confidence and feelings of self-worth.

The value of work is about self-esteem, self-management, and being able to provide life's necessities.

2. Give Your Teen Ownership of Their Money

Let your teen gradually take ownership of their money. As your teen gets older, give them more control over their financial future.

Every teen matures at a different rate. Use your teen's levels of maturity, responsibility, and decision making to gauge how much guidance your child needs when managing their money.

Of course, no matter your teen's age or maturity level, you must stay involved in your child's financial decisions, provide them with sound advice and wise guidance, and make sure they don't spend their college fund.

One way to gradually hand over control is to let your teen open their own bank account.

Many banks offer no-fee savings accounts and debit accounts for children. As your child's legal guardian, your name is also on the account.

You can open multiple accounts for your child (e.g., one account for long-term savings goals and one for everyday spending). If you decide to open a savings account or another type of interest-bearing account for your teen, talk to them about the benefits of accumulating compound interest. Teach your teen that they can earn interest on their money.

If possible, take your child to the bank and sit with them as the banker helps them open an account. If it is not possible to go to a bank, open the account online and let your child help you enter the necessary information.

Alternatives to bank accounts include money management apps for kids and debit cards for kids. Whatever method you decide (e.g., bank or app), the goal is to familiarize your teen with the process of opening an account and managing their money.

Let your teen put money they have earned into their account.

Earned money has intrinsic value. It is theirs. Let them take ownership of it.

3. Help Your Teen Track Their Credits and Debits

Being financially responsible means knowing how much money you have coming in, how much is going out, and where the money is going. In financial terms, these are credits, debits, and expense categories.

Teach your teen these three terms.

Credits are the money your teen receives. Credits include your teen's paycheck, money from doing chores or helping neighbors, and monetary gifts for birthdays, graduations, and holidays.

Debits are anything your teen spends money on. Debits include meals, toys, clothing, and any expenditures your teen has.

Expense categories are labels describing how or where money is spent. Expense categories include food, clothing, and entertainment.

Although a spreadsheet or pencil and paper are fine for tracking small expenditures or infrequent transactions, encourage your teen to use an app or bank account to automatically track their expenditures. Make sure you have access to the app or account so you and your teen can discuss their earning and spending behavior.

4. Help Your Teen Set Manageable Goals

Help your teen set manageable earning, spending, and savings goals.

Does your teen have a savings goal? Are their credits steady and recurring or sporadic? Are they managing their money well or do they need additional guidance?

Tell your teen they have to earn money to buy what they want. They have to save to reach their goals. They have to set reasonable expectations for what they can buy and how much money they can spend.

Encourage your teen to think about how their behavior affects their long-term goals. Let them learn from their mistakes.

If your teen spends all of their money, let them know it is gone. The Bank of Mom or Dad is closed.

Your teen must learn to live within their means. Teach them that, with time, they can recover from financial mistakes.

Help them learn their limits by tracking their money, making mistakes, and setting manageable goals.

5. Be Your Teen's Best Example

The best way to teach your teen about fiscal responsibility is for you yourself to be responsible. You are your teen's best example of what it means to value work, own your money, track expenses, and set manageable goals.

If you are proud of your job, the lessons you've learned about work over the years, or your ability to provide for your family, let your teen know. Discuss your career path, your triumphs, and your struggles.

Tell your teen how you learned, or are learning, to take ownership of your money. Discuss how you manage your accounts and why you entrust your money to a particular financial institution.

When you shop, explain prices to your teen. Discuss why you purchased one item instead of another. Explain that your credits, debits, and expense categories are different from your teen's. Let them know that their expenditures will change over time.

Talk about your financial goals for yourself, your family, and your teen. Discuss your plans for the future. Let your teen know where you have been financially, where you are now, and where you aspire to go.

Be a role model. Let them know you are striving to be financially responsible.

Answer your teen's questions, set a good example, and be honest about any financial mistakes you have made in the past.

Talk to your teen about money and what it takes to be financially responsible. If you don't, your teen will think money is a taboo topic. They won't talk to you when they have questions because you don't talk to them.

Who do you want your child to go to when they have money questions – their friend, the local loan shark, or you?

Teach your teen what they need to know about money and being financially responsible. Let them see you making smart financial decisions.

Their knowledge of money matters will help them throughout their lives.

Who knows, someday their knowledge may help you too.

PART III:
THE MINDSET

CHAPTER FOURTEEN

HOW TO PREPARE FOR AN HONEST
TALK ABOUT TOUGH FINANCIAL TIMES

Are you currently in a financial bind, but don't know how to talk to your family about it? Do you want to let your loved ones know that challenging financial times are in their future?

If you have never talked to your family about money, or the financial turmoil you are juggling behind the scenes, it is time to have an honest conversation.

Discussing money with family and friends is often viewed as a taboo subject. You'll hear people say, "No one needs to know about my money. It's personal. We may live in the same house, but I don't want you in my business."

Yes, your financial situation is personal. Yes, you have a right to retain your privacy. Yes, talking about your finances can be tough.

However, even with all of those truths, when your financial situation directly impacts someone else, that person deserves to know what's going on. They deserve to hear the truth so they can brace themselves for the future.

As a family, you can make a plan together.

Wouldn't it be great if you didn't have to carry the burden alone?

4 Tips to Prepare for a Tough Financial Discussion

1. Talk About Money

To complete a difficult task, the first action is always simple – begin. You must take the first step.

If you want your children to learn about saving, if you want your family to be prepared if you lose your job, if you want your spouse to be financially ready for your retirement, you have to talk about money.

Sadly, it is common for children and spouses to know nothing about their family's financial state until disaster strikes.

Have you heard of a family suddenly having to move because they can no longer pay their mortgage? Children having to change schools, or drop out, because their parents can no longer pay tuition? Children who have to suddenly expect less for holidays and birthdays because their parents no longer have the means to buy the things they used to buy? Spouses devastated because their husband or wife died and now the remaining spouse is destitute?

The stories of people being blindsided by life's financial changes are endless. The irony is that someone knew what was coming, and decided not to talk about it.

Talking about money doesn't have to be complicated. You make financial decisions every day. To begin your money discussions, talk about simple things. For example, discuss the prices of goods at the store and how those prices fit into your budget. Involve your entire family in grocery shopping, vacation planning, and household budgeting.

When talking to your children, you don't have to get into every detail regarding your income or the myriad of bills you pay. However, you should give your children a sense of whether you are living comfortably or stretched to the max. Include them in family discussions that pertain to them, their livelihood, and their wellbeing. Help your children understand what it means to make sound financial decisions.

When talking to your spouse, partner, or other adult remembers of your household, discuss your budget, plans for retirement, future career paths, bank accounts, life insurance, and the earning potential of your investments. Whether you have joint accounts or separate accounts, make sure you are on the same page when it comes to your finances.

Ongoing discussions will make it easier to talk about money when times are good and when they are bad.

Step one is simple. You have to do it.

If you want to get comfortable talking about money, open dialogue is the key.

2. Have Many Conversations

You don't have to discuss everything in one sitting. In fact, you should set a regular schedule for when you talk about your finances.

Should you talk with your family once a month, once a quarter, or every six months? Choose a timeframe that is right for you and your situation.

If you are new to having financial talks, talking every day is probably too much and talking once a year is probably too little. Begin with weekly financial conversations. Then, progress to monthly financial talks.

As you and your family become more comfortable talking about money – and everyone understands your financial situation – increase the amount of time between your scheduled financial talks (e.g., meet as a family every other month, then every three months).

It's okay to talk about your finances on a daily basis. However, if you are new to financial discussions, or nervous about talking with your family, a regular meeting schedule will help you with your plan to have open, honest talks. Put the dates on your family calendar and get started.

If you have a financial emergency, call a family meeting. Emergencies take precedence over your regularly scheduled talks. During an emergency, everyone needs to be made aware of the financial situation as soon as possible.

3. Don't Wait Until You Have an Emergency

If you wait to talk about money when you have an emergency, it's too late to talk.

Emotions are high. Stress levels are through the roof. Everyone wants to solve the problem now, and you may not be in an objective state of mind.

When the immediate goal is to deal with the emergency and get back to a state of normalcy, you're thinking in the moment and you may not be able to process the entire situation.

The sooner you talk about your money situation, plan for emergencies, and implement regularly scheduled conversations, the more confident you will feel about tackling emergencies.

4. Be Honest With Yourself and Your Loved Ones

If you are dealing with a tough financial situation right now, you may have to skip tips 1 through 3 and begin here, with tip 4.

Be honest about your financial situation.

An honest discussion is a teachable moment for you and your loved ones.

If you are struggling to provide for your family, share the story of your struggle with them. Work together to find a solution.

If you know hard financial times are on the horizon, let your family know what to expect and how upcoming changes will affect your future.

If you are embarrassed, depressed, or anxious about your financial situation, be honest with yourself about how you got where you are and what you will do to overcome your misfortune.

Write down what you want to say. Underline the most important points. Outline a preliminary plan of action.

If you become emotional and find it difficult to speak, look at your notes. Your written words will help you focus on telling your loved ones what they need to know.

Tell your family the truth. Speak calmly. Don't play the blame game, especially not in front of your children.

Develop a plan. Focus on the future. Put a plan in place that will prepare your family for your next tough financial dilemma.

If your financial news is upsetting, and your family is too angry, overwhelmed, or saddened to make a plan, consider taking a break for a few hours to give everyone a chance to process the news. Then, come together again as a family. Work together to develop a plan.

Your loved ones deserve to know about your family's financial state. Have an honest talk to prepare them for tough financial times.

CHAPTER FIFTEEN

4 MONEY MANAGEMENT TIPS
TO MAKE SHOPPING EASY

Are you ready to go shopping?

Here are four money management tips to help you budget your money, save more money, and earn easy money. Use these tips to make shopping a breeze.

1. Set Price Limits

Before you walk out the door, or begin shopping online, set price limits. Know what you plan to buy and how much you can afford to spend.

If you are buying gifts, use a gift giving guide and set a price limit for each gift. Write down each person's name. Put a dollar amount next to each name. Then track whether you stayed within your limits. Use the Order Your Life gift list to automatically keep track of your spending (https://orderyourlife. com/collections/money/products/gift-list-with-budget).

2. Price Match

Before you begin shopping, find out which retailers offer price matching. Whether you prefer shopping online or in-store, chances are you can find the best deal with price matching.

Online scenario: If you find the perfect item and it is beyond your price limit, add the item to your online cart and continue searching online for a better deal. By putting the item in your cart, you are essentially putting that item on hold and temporarily claiming it. Quickly conduct your search for a better deal, as most retailers only hold an item for 10-15 minutes before the hold expires and the item returns to available inventory. After your temporary hold ends, someone else can buy the item. If the item is still available, add it to your cart again to begin another temporary hold.

In-store scenario: If you are in the store when you find the perfect item, take out your phone, find the best deal, walk up to the counter, and ask if the store will match the price. Some retailers will match the price on the spot. Others may ask you to pay their price, then offer you a refund for the difference. Still others may ask you to fill out a form or speak with someone in customer service.

Most major retailers have price matching policies, and they are willing to match the prices of their major competitors. If the retailer matches the lower price, that's great. If the retailer does not match the lower price, you still win because you also have the option to get the best deal online. No matter what, remain friendly and treat the store representative with courtesy and kindness. You may learn about another deal or upcoming sale by being your charming self.

I bought it then found it for less scenario: If you buy the perfect item then find it for a lower price, you may be able to get a refund of the price difference. Whether you find the lower price online, in-store, at the retailer where you bought the item, or at one of the retailer's competitors, you may still be eligible for a refund.

Technically, when the price of an item drops and the retailer refunds you the difference, it is called a price adjustment. Whether the retailer calls it price matching or a price adjustment, the bottom line is that there is a window of opportunity in which you can get a lower price. Your time window can range anywhere from 24 hours to 30 days depending on the retailer. Thus, it is imperative that you make your request for a refund as soon as possible. You can get a price adjustment for an item purchased online or in-store. Contact the retailer's customer service department for assistance.

As a reminder, be kind to customer service representatives. They may go against policy "this one time" and give you the refund. (I always smile when this happens to me because, according to store policy, they do not have to give me a refund.)

3. Get Cash Back

Be economically savvy and get cash back on everything you buy. With apps, coupons, and rewards credit cards, it is easy to earn money on the money you spend. I have already discussed ways to save money with some of my favorite apps. Here I will discuss Ibotta, Rakuten, Paribus, and rewards credit cards.

Ibotta offers cash back rebates on groceries, apparel, furniture, restaurants, magazines, travel, and pretty much any item you can name. They have offers from hundreds of stores. With this app, you earn cash back on in-store and online purchases.

Rakuten (formerly known as Ebates) is another one of my favorite cash back sites. Like Ibotta, with Rakuten, you earn cash back for in-store and online purchases. Over 2000 retailers offer rebates through Rakuten.

Paribus (by Capital One) is a price tracking app that syncs with your email account, scans for online purchase receipts, and searches for lower prices on the items you have purchased. When a lower price is found, the app alerts you of the price drop and automatically requests a price adjustment on your behalf. The result, you get a refund.

If you use a credit card, make sure you use a rewards credit card. Each purchase should earn you cash back, points, or travel rewards such as miles. Discover (http://refer.discover.com/s/TYWANQUILA) is one of my favorite rewards cards because they offer excellent customer service as well as 5% cash back categories. In addition to earning a little extra when you use your card, credit cards offer the added benefits of being able to easily track your spending and dispute purchases. Note of caution – use your credit cards wisely. If you cannot afford an item, save until you can afford it or buy something you can afford. Be mindful of your price limits.

4. Embrace Free Shipping

Take advantage of free shipping and Free Shipping Day. Free Shipping Day was started in 2008 by Luke and Maisie Knowles. It is a promotional, mid-December holiday in which online retailers offer free shipping with guaranteed delivery by Christmas Eve. Participating retailers waive minimum purchase amounts, which means you can get free shipping no matter the price of your order.

Whenever you see a free shipping offer, read the retailer's free shipping details before you shop. For example, the retailer may offer free shipping on all items or only on specific items. Additionally, some retailers require free shipping coupons or promo codes while others automatically apply free shipping at checkout. Read the fine print and save money on shipping costs.

Now that you know how to navigate the shopping frenzy, let's simplify your life.

CHAPTER SIXTEEN

16 WAYS TO SIMPLIFY
YOUR LIFE

Although the first week of August is National Simplify Your Life Week, you can begin simplifying your life at any time. Let's start now.

This week, focus on the physical and psychological areas of your life that could use a little simplification. It is a time to refocus, declutter, and simplify. Use the next seven days to get rid of things that cause you stress and anxiety.

It's Physical and Mental

Simplifying your life is about the objects and things in your life as well as the mental, emotional, and spiritual elements that are unseen but vital to your existence. This week, choose one area of your life to simplify. For the next seven days, focus on that area with all your might.

Choose one area, because if you choose more than one, you're not really simplifying. Focus on one intention at a time. How would your simpler life look? How would your simpler life feel?

Ask Yourself

Are there areas in my home that cause me distress?

Are there thoughts and obsessions that keep me from enjoying my life?

Are there habits I can eliminate to simplify my life and decrease my stress?

What is one thing I can do this week to simplify my life?

Here are 16 ideas to help you get started.

1. Say no (to other people's demands and requests, social invitations, anything that's going to burden you and cause more problems than it's worth)

2. Declutter or clean for 15 minutes a day

3. Throw away, give away, or donate one item a day

4. Meditate for 15 minutes a day

5. Make a schedule (for work projects, social activities, family events)

6. Take a break from social media

7. Set a bedtime (and go to bed at that time no matter what)

8. Treat yourself to a destressing activity you enjoy (such as a massage, yoga, dancing, movie, dinner, live music, walking, hiking, karaoke, reading, a night out with friends)

9. Unsubscribe from services, lists, and websites you never use (such as magazines, email lists, streaming services, automatic text messages)

10. Subscribe to services that make your life easier (such as automatic deposits, automatic bill pay, automatic purchase and delivery of household goods)

11. Declutter and organize one room in your home (be

careful not to overextend yourself; do a little bit every day)

12. Declutter and organize one space in your home or office (such as your junk drawer, kitchen cabinet, kitchen counter, bedroom closet, living room table, kitchen table)

13. Declutter and organize one space in your office (such as your desk, file cabinet, desk drawer, bookshelf)

14. Donate, give away, or sell any clothes you have not worn in the last year

15. Before you go to bed, prepare for the next day (pack your lunch, pick out your clothes, put your backpack or suitcase near the front door)

16. Say no – This item is worth repeating because many of us feel obligated to say yes, even when saying no is the better, simpler option.

CHAPTER SEVENTEEN

5 WAYS TO HANDLE AN
OVERWHELMING SITUATION

L et's face it. Life happens, and it will continue happening for as long as we are lucky enough to draw breath.

Sometimes, we expect to be overwhelmed – in good ways and in bad (e.g., a wedding, the birth of a child, starting a new job, moving to a new home, retirement, the death of a loved one from a long-term illness).

Other times, no matter how prepared we think we are for life's surprises, we get slapped in the face with no warning – again, in good ways and in bad (e.g., a job promotion with additional responsibilities, an unexpected pregnancy, a separation or divorce, a sudden illness or injury, losing a job, encountering financial problems, a pandemic).

Unfortunately, the list of overwhelming bad situations overshadows the list of overwhelming good situations. These less than favorable circumstances may raise your stress level. You may feel your life is spinning out of control. Or you may reach a point of calm and clarity that shocks you with the obviousness of what you need to do to move forward.

The goal is to reach that point of clarity that propels you forward. Take actions that will help you survive and thrive, even in dire situations.

How do you cope with an overwhelming situation? What do you do when life happens?

How to Cope During Difficult Times

1. Don't Compare

Don't compare yourself to others. What people tell you, or what you see in their social media feeds, may not be the entire truth.

Most people have a desire to show their best selves to family, friends, and their public of adoring fans. They don't want you to see their pain or suffering. They don't want you to realize they are in the same situation as you, or possibly a worse situation than you.

No, they are not trying to deceive you. They just don't want you to see the other side. Most people want you to see them in their best light. It's understandable – they want you to see them as they wish to be seen, not necessarily as who they are.

They are doing fine. *They* have everything under control. *They* know how to deal with this situation. Do they really?

There are millionaires who can't pay their bills. There are happy couples who hate their other half. There are beautiful people who smile on the outside and cry on the inside.

Don't compare who you are to someone else. Although what you are going through may be similar to what someone else is experiencing, your situation is unique to you.

Do you really know what is going on in someone else's life? The only thing you can be 100% sure about is what's going on in your life.

2. Review Your Priorities

The things that were important to you before life happened may still be important. However, the order of your priorities may change.

Examine your goals and priorities. Have the top three items on your list changed? Do new circumstances require you to rearrange your priorities?

Visualize your new future and your new goals. Think about the changes you may need to make to accommodate your new situation. Do your best to maintain your priorities; keep them alive, no matter what.

You may have to rearrange, reestablish, or reinvent the most important things in your life.

Your life has changed. Your present may be vastly different from your past. Yet your future is still ahead of you. You must have priorities. They will anchor you.

3. Keep Doing What You Do

After reestablishing your priorities, continue doing what it takes to achieve your goals. Continue doing the things you enjoy. Continue striving to live the life you want to live, even if you are afraid you'll be kicked down again.

Dealing with an overwhelming situation does not mean you have to lose yourself. Yes, you may be temporarily lost as you work to envision your new life and the new you. You may need to take a break to regroup. You may need to take a break from everything and everyone. Yet know that the loss of yourself – of who you are when no one is looking – does not have to be permanent.

As soon as you are able, get back into your old (good) routines. You will be scared. You will be tired. You won't really feel you're ready. Does one ever feel ready?

Take baby steps. Then take giant leaps. You will feel comfort doing familiar things you love and enjoy. You will feel comfort knowing you are making progress towards your goals.

Keep doing what you do. Bring yourself back to your life one action at a time.

4. Acknowledge Change

Acknowledge that your life has changed, even if you aren't ready to accept the change. Acceptance (or at least the absence of vehement denial) will come with time.

Take obvious steps to recognize the change. Write it out in big, bold letters. Send yourself an email or text. Speak aloud; hear yourself say that change has come and you are here to meet it. Scream it from the rooftops. Call someone you trust, someone who will listen and not judge, someone who is genuinely concerned about the changes happening in your life.

Change is inevitable. If you're not changing, you're not growing.

Face change head on, because no matter what you do, change is going to happen.

5. Make an Unmanageable Situation Manageable

There are many roadmaps to the same place. When one road is blocked, take another road or forge a new path. When you find yourself in an overwhelming, seemingly unmanageable situation, don't change the goal, change the method of reaching the goal.

Make an unmanageable situation manageable. Take time, money, people, effort, and motivation into consideration.

- Adjust your timeline. What do you need to do to achieve your goal within a shorter, or longer, timeframe?

- Modify your financial strategy. What can you do to save more money, pay off debt faster, or earn extra income?

- Ask for help. Lean on your support network to get you through tough times. Who truly cares about you? Who will provide a strong shoulder in your time of need?

- Put forth more effort. Can you contribute more effort and energy to the situation? Will more effort make the situation more manageable?

- Put forth less effort. Are you dedicating too much time and energy? Are you fighting for a lost cause or increasing your stress unnecessarily?

- Modify your motivation. Are you motivated to tackle change? What do you need to do to increase your drive and energy to handle your current situation?

There are many ways to get to the same place. How you navigate the twists and turns is up to you.

Be willing to take a few detours, or draw an entirely different map.

Bonus: Give Yourself Time

In the moment, any situation can feel endless, as if it will never go away, as if normalcy is beyond your reach.

You may cry. You may scream. You may wonder why this has happened to you.

You may doubt. You may deny. You may not understand why this has happened to you.

Give yourself time to crumble, to question, to rail, to criticize, to cope, to understand, to rise, to rebuild.

Truth – your life will not be the same. Have you grown from your experience?

Truth – *you* will not be the same. Are you stronger, better, braver for your experience?

Truth – life if what you make of it. Do you have the skills you need to cope when life happens?

Learn. Live. Love. Grow. Survive. Thrive.

Know that this too shall pass.

CHAPTER EIGHTEEN

6 TIPS TO HELP YOU MAKE A
TOUGH DECISION

As you simplify your life and navigate difficult situations, you may be faced with some tough decisions.

Are you overwhelmed? Do you need help deciding what to do? You are not alone.

Every day, we are faced with dozens of decisions. There are easy, mundane decisions. Should I have coffee or tea? Should I walk another lap around the track? Which socks should I wear?

There are life-altering decisions. Should I attend the local college or the one out of state? Should I move to the city or stay where I am? Which job should I take?

With so many options, it is easy for us to become overwhelmed and indecisive. Here are 5 tips to help you weigh your options and make a tough decision.

1. Be Specific.

Ask yourself a specific question. In that question, give yourself specific options.

Why bother being specific? If you don't know what you are trying to decide, it will be harder to make a decision. If you don't know your options, you may make a decision that does not solve your problem.

Here are examples of vague and specific questions.

Scenario: You have applied to five universities. You have been accepted to two universities, ABC and XYZ.

- Vague: Where should I go to school?
- Specific: Should I go to ABC University or XYZ University?

For the vague question, you can decide you'd like to go to LMNOP University because that's where all of your friends are going. LMNOP is a great school. However, it is not on your list of options.

Deciding to go to LMNOP University does not solve your problem because you were not accepted to LMNOP. The question with specific options will help you reach a decision that solves your problem.

2. Stay True to Your Values.

Make sure your decision is in line with your values. Stay true to who you are and think about what you truly want. If you go against your values, you may feel unhappy. You may even regret your decision.

Take a moment to think about a time when you did the opposite of what you believed. How did you feel? Were you excited at first, then miserable later? Did you keep thinking about the decision long after it had been made?

No matter what decision you make, be true to yourself. Be your authentic self. Uphold your values.

3. Talk It Out.

Talk to a trusted friend or advisor. Make sure the person is someone who will keep your confidences, is trustworthy, and gives sound advice.

We all have friends who are great to talk to and willing to agree with whatever we say. However, for those tough decisions, you need to talk to someone who will tell you the truth, whether you want to hear it or not.

People who love you enough to be honest with you (and gentle with your feelings) are rare and valuable creatures. Hang on to these people. Listen to what they have to say.

I know you're thinking, "I don't want to hear the truth. I want someone to decide for me." This is your decision. Own it. At the end of the day, you have to be the person who decides. You will be the one who lives with the consequences.

Talk. Listen. Then make your own decision.

4. Write It Down.

Write your options down. Make a list of pros and cons for each of those options.

Writing down your specific questions, options, pros, and cons will help you think about what you should do. Rate the importance of each pro and con on a scale of 1-10. A rating of 1 means that item is not at all important. A rating of 10 means it is extremely important. After you have entered all of your items, add up the ratings for your pros. Then add up the ratings for your cons.

To quickly add up your pros and cons, use the Order Your Life Pros and Cons spreadsheet (https://orderyourlife.com/collections/excel-spreadsheets/products/pros-and-cons). The spreadsheet automatically calculates your totals. There are also colorful rating bars that move as you add items and ratings to the list.

Seeing your pros and cons written down will help you weigh your options. Rating each item will help you see what is important to you. By writing your options down, you will be better able to make a decision that is true to your values, weighs all your options, and gives you the information you need to make a well-thought-out decision.

5. Decide.

Eventually, you have to make a decision. Use all the information you have to make that decision.

Procrastinating and worrying will only lead to more worry. Chances are, the longer you wait, the more anxious you will become. Making a decision may ease your anxiety and give you a sense of calm.

There are no guarantees that things will turn out perfectly. Yet, after making a decision, you will feel the proverbial weight lift off of your shoulders.

6. Celebrate.

After you make a decision, congratulate yourself. Celebrate making it through the decision-making process. Although you make dozens of decisions every day, decision-making can be hard. Celebrate your new skills and rejoice in your decisiveness. Then, put your plan into action.

Use your newfound knowledge to achieve an economically savvy mindset. Wealth and financial wellness are within your reach. Decide what you want. Go forth and be economically savvy!

ADDITIONAL RESOURCES & INFORMATION

ABOUT THE AUTHOR

Dr. Tywanquila Walker is the CEO and founder of Order Your Life. She has a bachelor's degree from Vanderbilt University and a Ph.D. from Cornell University. To learn more about Dr. Walker and Order Your Life, visit OrderYourLife.com.

Books by Tywanquila Walker
Order Your Life Moving Guide
Economically Savvy

ECONOMICALLY SAVVY RESOURCES

Visit my website to get links to all the economically savvy resources listed in this book. I created a page specifically for Economically Savvy readers. Use the full URL or the shortened URL.

Full URL
https://orderyourlife.com/blogs/blog/economically-savvy-resources

Shortened URL
https://bit.ly/3mxFVPK

GET EARLY ACCESS TO THE LATEST CONTENT

Would you like early access to the latest Order Your Life content? Join our community at OrderYourLife.com and follow Order Your Life on social media.

Connect on Social Media

Facebook

https://www.facebook.com/OrderYourLifeLLC

Twitter

https://twitter.com/OrderYour_Life

Pinterest

https://www.pinterest.com/OrderYour_Life

YouTube

https://www.youtube.com/@orderyourlife

Blog

https://orderyourlife.com/blogs/blog

REVIEW THIS BOOK

What did you think of this book? Your honest review is appreciated.

Please let others know what you think about *Economically Savvy*. Your opinion matters, and I greatly appreciate your honest review. Thank you!